GIANT BEAST CINEMA

A MONSTROUS MOVIE GUIDE

Editors: Steven Peros and Mark Bailey

Co-Editor: Steven B. Orkin

Reviews by Larry Blamire, Justin Humphreys, Tracy Mercer, Mike Peros, Steven Peros, and Brian R. Solomon

DEDICATION

To the parents who let us watch monster movies.

Giant Beast Cinema - A Monstrous Movie Guide

©2023 Steven Peros

Published in the USA by:

BearManor Media
1317 Edgewater Dr. #110
Orlando FL 32804
www.BearManorMedia.com

ISBN-10: 979-8-88771-260-4 Giant Beast Cinema
ISBN-13: 979-8-88771-261-1 Giant Beast Cinema hb

Art, Design, and Layout: Mark Bailey

TABLE OF CONTENTS

  TOC 

   TOC  

Introduction

STEVEN PEROS

When the previous volume in this series, *Giant Bug Cinema - A Monster Kid's Guide*, was in its final stages, I discovered that my childhood friend since junior high school, Steve Orkin, was one of its editors. Never one to put pride before a monster, I guilted him into reaching out to the book's creator, Mark Bailey, to see if there was any way I could contribute. As fate would have it, Mark did have an assignment for me, Ray Harryhausen's *First Men in the Moon*. Again, since a Monster Kid knows no shame, I pitched a second movie which I saw was not contained in the Table of Contents: *Quatermass and the Pit*, a brilliant sci-fi/horror classic from Hammer Films, and thus, found myself writing two chapters.

After *Giant Bug Cinema* hit #1 on Amazon for Horror Movie Books, I pitched to Mark the idea of a follow-up, accounting for giant monsters that were not bugs. Fortunately, not only did Mark think it was a good idea, so did Ben Ohmart at BearManor Media. Mark came up with the title, cover, and design, Steve Orkin came on board to copy-edit, and I assembled a team of five writers to join me. All had either published writing in this specific arena or engaged eloquently about horror/sci-fi movies in other outlets.

After Mark Bailey and I agreed on the 33 movies for this book, each writer was given a list to choose from. However, in several cases, I put a pin in certain titles that I felt were tailor-made for specific writers. For example, I knew that *The Magic Sword* was a particularly special movie for filmmaker and historian, Larry Blamire. Despite writing lauded biographies on fine thespians, my brother Mike Peros lists *Konga* among his cinematic comfort food, so that was a no-brainer. I just knew I wanted a female take on *Attack of the 50 Foot Woman*, and Tracy Mercer delivered the goods. *The Thief of Bagdad* is one of the learned

Justin Humphreys' most coveted movies, so of course that title was his. Finally, I wanted a Japanese giant monster movie (or kaiju) expert to write about the majority of those films in our roster, so I cold-called Brian R. Solomon, based on the success of his *Godzilla FAQ*, and could not be happier with the results. As for me, five of my eight titles hold a very special place in my still-beating Monster Kid's heart.

As the chapters came in, I knew we had bet on the right five horses. Each one contains the unique voice, vast memory bank, and idiosyncratic sense of humor of its distinctly mad author. And there's not a bad penny in the bunch. These are all movies I had watched many times and yet each one of these writers made me see them in a way I had not seen them before. I know each chapter will do the same for you.

Now allow me to explain our entirely random rules, designed so that this book didn't become a giant beast in and of itself. Essentially, we decided that a "Giant Beast" would be defined as an existing life form that is a beast because it *isn't supposed to be giant*. That allowed us to eliminate the myriad dinosaur and Godzilla movies, and focus on big apes, octopi, men, women, teenagers, crabs, and of course mollusks, to name a few of the stars of this book. Even *Gamera*, who I adore and champion, isn't here because while he is indeed a giant turtle, he also flies and breathes fire. *Gamera* is his own thing, and that thing is giant from the outset.

Finally, as with *Giant Bug Cinema*, we are exploring this arena only up until the accepted end of the "Monster Kid Era" — 1968 (although we did sneak in one worthy retro entry from 1969 because it was too enjoyable to resist). But rest assured, we are already in discussions to bring our readers second volumes of both *Giant Bug Cinema* and *Giant Beast Cinema*, which will take us into the gonzo 1970's, 1980's and beyond.

My great thanks to Mark for his guidance and book design, Steven for his indefatigable eagle-eye and always-on-the-money suggestions, Ben for his unwavering support, and the five exceptional writers who brought their evident enthusiasm and A-Game to every chapter. I know you will step way from this book with a new level of appreciation for Giant Beasts you only thought you knew.

But then again, can one ever really know a killer shrew?

Steven Peros is an award-winning filmmaker, playwright, and comic-book writer whose debut Rondo Award-nominated graphic novel, *Stoker & Wells* (available on *Amazon* and *Comixology*), is being developed for TV by the former President of *Marvel Studios* at his company, *Amasia*. Steven wrote *The Cat's Meow*, starring Kirsten Dunst and directed by the legendary Peter Bogdanovich, sold one-hour dramas to *NBC*, *MTV*, and written for *AMC*'s Emmy-winning series, *The Lot*. Steven was a writer on *Disney's Around the World in 80 Days*, starring Jackie Chan, and wrote *A Country Christmas Story*, featuring Dolly Parton. Steven is also a film historian who wrote chapters for *Giant Beast Cinema* (BearManor) and articles for *MovieMaker*, *Village Voice*, *Scr(i)pt*, and others. He has contributed BluRay commentary tracks for many classic films and is an avid 16mm film and movie poster collector, many of which prominently feature giant beasts (five from this book alone!). For his social media links and contact information, please visit *stevenperos.com*.

Justin Humphreys is a writer, film historian, and curator. He has published four books, including the *Rondo Award*-winning *The Dr. Phibes Companion*. His most recent book, *George Pal: Man of Tomorrow*, is the authorized biography of the *Academy Award*-winning director/producer/animator who fathered the modern science fiction film, and it was prepared with the George Pal Estate's full cooperation. Copies are available at *bearmanormedia.com*. He regularly records audio commentaries and appears on-camera in BluRay special features, and has worked extensively with movie props, costumes, and other memorabilia for *Bonhams Auctions* and *The Academy Museum of*

Motion Pictures, among others. His articles have appeared in magazines like *Rue Morgue*, *L'Ecran Fantastique*, *Filmfax*, and *True West*. He also sincerely wishes that all weaselly, pedantic reviewers online — not the nice ones: the weaselly, pedantic kind — would be gobbled up by the giant monsters featured in this book, and that he gets to watch.

Larry Blamire is a writer, director, actor, artist, and playwright known for feature films, *The Lost Skeleton of Cadavra*, *Trail of the Screaming Forehead*, *The Lost Skeleton Returns Again*, and *Dark and Stormy Night*, and is writer-creator of the *Mark Time Award*-winning *Big Dan Frater* audio series. This unrepentant Monster Kid contributes to numerous Blu-ray commentaries and is the proud recipient of three *Rondo Awards*, including for his *Star Turn* column in *Video Watchdog Magazine*. His books (at *Lulu.com*) include *Doc Armstrong: Suburb at the Edge of Never*, two western-horror collections (*Tales of the Callamo Mountains*), and volumes of surreal cartoons. Larry won the Boston Theatre Critics Circle Award for Best Actor and is a published playwright whose *Robin Hood* has been performed worldwide. His epic, *Steam Wars* (*steamwars.com*), is about to be unleashed in graphic novel form, and he regularly writes/illustrates for Onyx Path RPG's. Larry is currently developing a comic, *Flapjack Alley*, and can be found hiding under his own name on Facebook, Twitter, and Instagram.

Mike Peros is the author of the recent, well-received Hollywood biographies *Dan Duryea: Heel with a Heart* and *Jose Ferrer: Success and Survival*, both published by the University Press of Mississippi. He also writes film reviews for *NoHoArtsDistrict.com*, where he tries to steer readers to films that might have otherwise escaped their attention (while also occasionally reviewing studio blockbusters). When he's not watching or writing about movies, Mike can be found in Brooklyn as the English Department Chair at Bishop Loughlin Memorial High School. Perhaps his favorite movie monster is Christopher Plummer's unsettling, all-too-inhuman psychopath in *The Silent Partner*.

Tracy Mercer is an *Emmy*-nominated TV and film executive-turned-producer who has worked on projects, including Ang Lee's *Hulk*, *Aeon Flux*, *Invictus*, *Five Flights Up* and the *CBS* hit series, *Madam Secretary*. She is also a co-host of the irreverent film buff comedy podcast, *My Favorite Shtty Movie*, which can be watched on both its Facebook and Twitter show pages, with the audio version available for downloading anywhere you find your podcasts. Tracy is a third generation Angeleno and second generation cinephile who was weaned on equal parts Universal Monster films, 1950's sci-fi classics, and campy midnight movies. Among her proudest achievements: being sent to the principal's office in 3rd grade for making her flip-book version of the *Alien* chest-burster scene and earning her brown belt in Tae Kwon Do. She currently resides in Los Angeles with her rescue mutt, Snake Plissken.

Brian R. Solomon is a pop culture and film writer with more than 25 years of experience. He's the author of six books on sports and entertainment, including the award-winning *Blood and Fire: The Unbelievable Real-Life Story of Wrestling's Original Sheik*, as well as *Godzilla FAQ*, the comprehensive reference guide for the Big G. His love affair with *kaiju* began back in the late 70's thanks to the monster movie marathons on WOR Channel 9 in New York City, and he'll always have a soft spot for *Godzilla vs. The Smog Monster* and, yes, *Godzilla's Revenge*. Brian has also worked extensively within the pro wrestling business, including seven years with *WWE*, spending his time among a different breed of angry, fighting giants. He's also a podcaster and reporter, as well as an English teacher with a master's specialization in Shakespeare. He is the proud father of three, and lives in Trumbull, Connecticut with his wife and youngest son.

What more can be said that hasn't already been stated so eloquently? I am the carnival barker/used car salesman who conceived, project managed, and designed the original *Giant Bug Cinema - A Monster Kid's Guide*. I'm now thrilled to see the fruits of my creative labor evolve into a new and wonderful collaborative venture! It's very exciting to be working with the two Steves again because they were an integral part of our original success. Steve Orkin is a longtime friend and skilled writer who's always had my back, while Steve Peros is a more recent acquaintance who has energized this publishing endeavor to heights I could only dream of. The new contributors are accomplished in their own writing careers, incredibly entertaining, and very funny. I hope the readers enjoy their input as much as I did. This time around, I focused on the roles of designer and occasional advisor. I'm immensely pleased with the level of collaboration and creativity that has been offered for the sole purpose of making this the best giant monster reading experience possible (until we make the next one). I live in the great state of New Jersey with my brilliant and lovely wife Kara (Hrabosky) and our feline overlords Ella, Griffin, and Roxie.

A Note From
Steven B. Orkin

It's been a profound pleasure and a privilege (or, to quote the great Tom Waits, "a preasure and a plivilege") to lend my editing talents to this wonderful project. First and foremost, it's been fun and meaningful to work with my two near-lifelong friends, Steven Peros and Mark Bailey. My respect, affection, and admiration for them, both personally and professionally, cannot be overstated. Though I didn't get to meet the amazing writers of the essays herein (except for Steve and Mike, of course), I felt I got a sense of them through their work. I found it deeply gratifying and satisfying to refine their words ever-so-slightly and thereby bring greater clarity to them. I learned a lot about the films (many of which I haven't seen but now hope to), and the film business that facilitated them. The writers have all accomplished exactly what they set out to do: inform and entertain, each in their own unique voice, and that is no small thing.

I'm a writer in my own right, with a passion for storytelling and the craft of writing. In addition to my co-editing credits on *Giant Bug Cinema - A Monster Kid's Guide* and this work, I am the author of the novella, *Susie*, available on Amazon, and was a winner of Stephen King's *On* Writing contest, from his wonderful memoir / writing guide of the same name. I also moderate a local writing group here on Long Island. You can learn more about me at my website: *https://starren. wixsite.com/stevenorkin.*

1933

STEVEN PEROS

As one of the editors of this book, I should make my bias known: *King Kong* is my favorite movie of all time. It is a film I watched yearly as a boy on New York's WOR-TV Channel 9 during the Thanksgiving holidays. In those pre-VCR Dark Ages, I used my brother's tape recorder and made an audio recording of the movie on two one-hour cassette tapes (hitting the "stop" button during the commercial breaks). I listened to them over and over, like an old-time radio show (or a current-time podcast), reliving the fantastical adventure in my head. This was followed by a VHS tape, then a DVD, and finally, a 16mm film print which I screen for young and old. From its transporting score by Max Steiner, to all its charming performances, to the groundbreaking level of artistic craftsmanship at every level, *King Kong* far exceeded anything audiences at the time could possibly have expected to behold when the lights went down in 1933.

Declaring it my favorite movie is not the same as saying I believe it is "the best movie" of all time nor "the finest movie" of all time. But we all have *favorite* movies. They are usually films we discovered in our formative years, somewhere between childhood and sixteen years of age which, for some inexplicable (or explicable) reason, mean something to us like no other. Director Guillermo del Toro once tweeted about "one-sock movies", which he defined as "you're getting dressed - you catch it on TV and sit down (one sock in hand) and watch it until the end." We're glued to that old friend who makes us happy, place life on hold, and the idea of going out is now delayed or a thing of the past. That is not only what *King Kong* is to me but to many of you and to many great filmmakers, from *Lord of the Rings'* Peter Jackson on down, who filmed his own ambitious remake in 2005.

I would be shocked if anyone reading this requires a plot recap, but here goes regardless: adventure movie producer, Carl Denham (Robert Armstrong), follows a secret map to an uncharted island where some sort of "god" named "Kong" is purported to live. He brings along an actress who's hit hard times named Ann Darrow (Fay Wray), and she falls for Denham's first mate, Jack Driscoll (Bruce Cabot). Kong turns out to be a 50-foot-tall gorilla who, in turn, falls for Ann and, thanks to the interference of the local native tribe, takes her into his jungle where he fights dinosaurs to protect her and disposes of sailors, all before being captured by Denham, put on display in a Broadway theater, escaping, and snatching Ann once again. Kong climbs the recently-opened Empire State Building where, after placing Ann down to keep her out of harm's way, he is shot to death by bi-planes, although Denham's final words clarify, "It wasn't the airplanes. It was Beauty killed the Beast."

Despite my love for this film, or rather because of it, I delayed writing about *King Kong*, until my other eight chapters were complete because I knew it would be the hardest. I wanted to write something that had its own place beyond the myriad books and articles that have been written over the last 50+ years, usually (and rightfully) focusing on the film's complex special effects and the enduring power of its "beauty and the beast" scenario. 2023 marks King Kong's 90th Anniversary. And since it is the Mommy & Daddy of every Giant Beast Movie in this book, an interesting question to ponder in our first chapter is: Who is

King Kong's Mommy & Daddy?

As a member of the Writers Guild of America, which as I write this chapter is on strike for fairer contracts, I realized that for all I know about this movie, for as many times as I have watched it, I couldn't definitively answer the question of *King Kong*'s complex authorship. The opening credits read as follows:

Screen Play by
JAMES CREELMAN and RUTH ROSE
From an idea conceived by
EDGAR WALLACE and MERIAN C. COOPER

How is one to interpret that original credit block? The use of the word "and" as opposed to the ampersand ("&") implies that these screenwriters worked separately, meaning that Creelman and Rose were not a writing team but rather two individual writers who wrote their drafts of the screenplay alone and at different times.

The project had its genesis as far back as 1929, when nature docudrama director/producer, Merian C. Cooper, became simultaneously fascinated by gorillas (which had only recently been introduced to western culture) and 10-foot long Komodo Dragons. Cooper wanted to do a movie that teamed these two beasts. He wrote notes and ideas, but the idea of a giganticizing the gorilla didn't surface until 1931, when Cooper accepted a job with famed producer David O. Selznick, then head of RKO, who was intrigued by the gorilla story but needed Cooper to examine his studio's development slate and help make tough recommendations as to which projects to ax, due the hard financial hits of the Great Depression.

The first RKO movie Cooper canceled was the over-budget *Creation*, a dinosaur-filled adventure which was the handiwork of special effects pioneer, Willis O'Brien. He and his director, Harry Hoyt, had had a huge hit six years earlier with the silent film, *The Lost World*, based on Arthur Conan Doyle's novel about a group of explorers who discover an unknown world filled with dinosaurs, capture one, and bring it to London, where it escapes and wreaks havoc (sound familiar?). But Cooper was not impressed with their follow-up movie's blah storyline, which to him felt like a relic from the silent movie era. However, the special effects dazzled him, resulting in Cooper offering O'Brien a job to create *Kong*'s special effects, the gorilla now growing in size from

12-feet to 18-feet in order to fight dinosaurs rather than a relatively puny Komodo Dragon.

In order to convince the nervous shareholders at RKO about the expensive *Kong*'s potential, Selznick gave Cooper and O'Brien funds to produce test footage and conceptual art. While this was happening, Cooper flew well-known British mystery writer, Edgar Wallace, to Hollywood in late November, 1931, to write a first draft. Wallace wrote to his wife about Cooper on Christmas Day: "We talked over the big animal play we are going to write, or, rather, I am writing and he is directing. He has just had an approval from New York, and I am going to turn him out a scenario." Apparently, the deal made with Wallace was Cooper would advise, consult, discuss ideas, but Wallace would write the actual screenplay, not unlike how Alfred Hitchcock would work with his hand-picked screenwriters on the movie ideas he generated. However, unlike Hitchcock, Cooper wanted to share on-screen writing credit, and Wallace complied. Sadly, after writing his first draft, called "The Beast", dated January 5th 1932, Wallace took ill in Hollywood and died from the combined forces of pneumonia and diabetes on February 10th, before completing his revised draft. The project would go through many titles, largely due to RKO not liking the single-word title, "Kong", proposed by Cooper. Other titles during development include "The Eighth Wonder" and the briefly considered, "King Ape".

In Wallace's script, "Danby" Denham is a big-game hunter searching for a sea serpent that his Captain swears he once saw off the coast of the mysterious Vapour Island. Their path intersects with a lifeboat full of escaped convicts, who have taken a woman named Shirley hostage, and all find themselves on the uncharted island. The "sea serpent" soon appears in the form of a Brontosaurus that comes out of the sea. Later, an 18-foot gorilla bursts out of the jungle to protect Shirley from being raped by one of the convicts. Kong takes Shirley captive, fights a Tyrannosaurus to protect her, and brings her to his cave. She is saved by John, a convict who has fallen in love with her. Kong chases them back to shore where Denham uses gas bombs to subdue the ape, who they take back to New York and put on display in Madison Square Garden. Once there, Kong escapes, wreaks havoc, recaptures Shirley, climbs the Empire State Building, is buzzed by bi-planes, but is killed by a lightning strike.

Some will read this first draft script summary and think that clearly Wallace deserves credit, but others might take issue. What of Denham's character being a movie producer? What's with the boatload of convicts? Where's the romance? Where's the 50-foot beast? Where are the natives, the great wall, and the Broadway unveiling? Aren't these the makings of *King Kong*? Merian Cooper would concur, saying years later, "Edgar Wallace didn't write any of *Kong*, not one bloody word … I'd promised him credit and so I gave it to him." But Wallace supporters think this unfair, pointing to the story elements of the script as evidence, which has recently been published for the first time.

This leads each of us to ask ourselves what is it about *King Kong* that makes it *King Kong* for us? If it's that an overgrown gorilla is captured on a dinosaur-filled island, brought to New York, falls in love with a woman, climbs a tall building, and is killed, then you're in Camp Wallace. But if it's Kong at 50-feet tall being the object of interest of a Cooper-esque movie producer, then you'd have to look to James Creelman, who rewrote Wallace from scratch. You'd also have to consider Willis O'Brien's "authorship", who encouraged Cooper to push his story ideas in specific ways based on what he could achieve with his special effects. And yet, if you are fascinated by the natives and the great wall that protects them from Kong, that was the writing of the uncredited Horace McCoy, who came on board when Creelman (who didn't like those ideas) had to return to work on RKO's *The Most Dangerous Game* for Cooper and Selznick. Finally, if your love of *King Kong* is the sweetness of the Ann and Jack courtship, the fun dialogue, the charm of Denham, and the fast pace (reportedly, a result of streamlining Creelman's wordy prose and dialogue), you can thank the final screenwriter, Ruth Rose (wife of the movie's co-director, Ernest B. Schoedsack), who modeled Ann on herself, Jack on her husband, and Denham on Cooper.

Ultimately, just as we refer to movies as "Alfred Hitchcock films" even though he didn't write them, Cooper dreamed up the initial idea and handpicked everyone who contributed. Does this mean Cooper deserves writing credit? Directors and producers give creative instructions to costume designers and cinematographers yet do not expect to share on-screen credit with them. Regardless, Cooper's name should have come before Edgar Wallace in the current "Conceived by" credit, since the order of names is indicative of who worked first, second, etc. And while it may be technically accurate that no writing from Wallace's screenplay survived in the final shooting script, his creative collaboration with Cooper is engrained in the finished product. Perhaps as the years went on, it galled Cooper that he agreed to take second billing to Wallace, which was done less for ethical reasons than commercial ones, due to Wallace's immense popularity and the impressiveness of his name, which was always in larger typeface than Cooper's name in the poster art.

After taking this deep dive into the conception and writing history of *King Kong*, the final on-screen credit should probably have been "Screenplay by Edgar Wallace and James Creelman and Ruth Rose, from a story idea by Merian C. Cooper". This apex of giant monster movies is the hairy lovechild of a giant family of writers and artists. *King Kong* would not exist in its present iconic form without the unique contribution of each one of them, with Merian C. Cooper as their never-say-die patriarch. And for that, we should all be forever grateful.

THE SON OF KONG

1933

STEVEN PEROS

After the boffo box-office of *King Kong* in March of 1933, Merian C. Cooper was asked to fast-track a sequel that would be ready for Christmas. Nine months was an extraordinarily tight schedule for a special effects-filled movie, especially since there wasn't even a whiff of a screenplay, but Cooper, a fighter-pilot hero of World War I, was the very definition of an adventurer, so he said yes more often than he said no, and this was no exception.

One month earlier, David O. Selznick had left RKO, so Cooper was promoted to VP of Production, which meant he was wearing two hats: studio executive and movie producer, which then, as now, was not typical. Given the demands of running the studio, Cooper took an Executive Producer credit, relinquished co-directing *The Son of Kong*, and gave the solo job to his longtime directing partner, Ernest B. Schoedsack.

Ruth Rose (Schoedsack's wife) was the final screenwriter on *King Kong* and began writing the sequel, which assumed a *King Kong* scope, with Denham returning to Skull Island in search of treasure, entering the jungle through the shattered Great Wall, further confrontation with the natives, rampaging herds of dinosaurs, and the appearance of King Kong's offspring, often referred to as Kiko in movie books, though no such name is given to Little Kong in the film itself (I suspect it is the name used in Rose's screenplay).

Unlike today's *Marvel* and *Star Wars* sequels, back then, sequels were considered a quickie cash-grab for diminishing returns. Cooper was told he could have only $250,000 to make the film, which was less than half the budget of *King Kong*. This sequel philosophy continued for decades, notably with Fox's four sequels to 1968's *Planet of the Apes*, each entry made for a lower price-tag than the one that preceded it. Working again with special effects genius, Willis O'Brien, Cooper and Rose cut and downsized her epic script. Gone were the larger set pieces, the rampaging herd of dinosaurs, and the native village. While it took over a half-hour of *King Kong*'s 100-minute running time for the 50-foot gorilla to appear, here, it takes until two-thirds of the movie's scant 69 minutes for the first appearance of 12-foot Kiko, or any giant beast.

Denham, Captain Englehorn (Frank Reicher), and Charlie the Cook (Victor Wong) leave the US to hide from Denham's Kong-related lawsuits and news of a grand jury indictment. After anchoring in fictitious Dakang (Catalina Island doubling for its port scenes), they bump into a character who was only referenced in *Kong*, Captain Helstrom (John Marston), who had given Denham the original map they followed to Skull Island. When down-on-his luck Helstrom suggests that Denham should cut him in on his Kong profits, he agrees, offering 50% of his lawsuits and indictment. That's when Helstrom asks if they also retrieved the island's hidden treasure. As this is news to Denham, they all agree to head back to Skull Island.

What Denham doesn't know is that Helstrom has just killed Peterson (Clarence Wilson), the owner of a local low-rent vaudeville show, in a drunken fight. Denham and Englehorn had taken in the show earlier that evening (a bizarre troop of performing musical monkeys eats up what feels like several minutes of screen time) where Denham developed a soft spot for the guitar-strumming singer, billed as "La Belle Helene" (Peterson's daughter, played by Helen Mack). The opening credits name her "Hilda", but nowhere in the movie is that name ever said (Denham affectionately calls her "kid" throughout). Other opening credit head-scratchers include the title, boldly proclaiming *The Son of Kong*. Yet in all 1933 poster art (as well as DVD and blu-ray covers), and now for posterity, the movie is referred to without the article, as simply *Son of Kong*. Finally, Ruth Rose has a solo "Story by" credit, but oddly, there is no "Screenplay by" or "Written by" credit. All of this amplifies how fast this movie was cobbled together. Now back to our story…

After Denham and "a skeleton crew" (a.k.a. fewer extras to pay than on *King Kong*) set sail for Skull Island, the sailors discover that Hilda is a stowaway, wanting justice for her father. In an effort to rid himself of Hilda, Helstrom tells the crew how a dozen men were killed on Denham's previous trip to Skull Island. They mutiny and send Denham, Englehorn, Hilda, and Charlie off on a rowboat. When Helstrom starts barking orders seconds later, the socialist crew throw him overboard, declaring there will be no captains! Denham begrudgingly saves the traitor's life.

The quintet row themselves to Skull Island where a dozen natives (including the chief, once again played by Noble Johnson) come to the beach, therefore eliminating the need for a native village set. When the natives send them away with their spears, they dock elsewhere. As Hilda and Denham look for treasure, they encounter Little Kong, albino, playful, 12-feet tall, and stuck in quicksand. Feeling guilty about the death of his pop, Denham aids Little Kong in his escape. Now begins the final 26 minutes, with one stop-motion effects sequence after another: Little Kong (who frequently mugs cutely for the camera) fights a giant bear and a dinosaur, while nearby, Englehorn, Helstrom, and Charlie are trapped in a cave by a Styracosaurus. Inexplicably, the giant beasts are all in Little Kong's weight class, unlike the much larger beasts who duked it out with his 50-foot pop. Clearly, Denham & Company rowed their boat to the kid's section of Skull Island. The treasure is ultimately found, which is a surprise to Helstrom, who had made the story up in order to get out of town on Denham's boat. But karma arrives when Helstrom attempts to flee in their rowboat, cueing a sea beast to rear its head and gobble him up.

That's when *deus ex machina* kicks in as a convenient earthquake *and* tropical storm decide to strike for no other reason than the end credits are fast approaching. The island crumbles and sinks with only Little Kong and Denham left on its highest peak. The little guy gets his leg caught in the shifting earth but manages to hold only his hand safely above the waves with Denham in his grasp (a touching recall of Fay Wray in poppa's clutches) long enough for Englehorn, Charlie, and Hilda to row close enough to get him. And with a last wave goodbye, the son of Kong disappears beneath the surface forever.

The Son of Kong is an enjoyable, well-acted, if inconsequential film. For all its on-screen light-heartedness (the trailer's oddly-punctuated tagline declares: "A Human - lovable laughable beast!"), the film must have been a sobering experience for its two famous creative forces: Cooper and O'Brien. Following the validation of *King Kong*'s great success, shooting *The Son of Kong* brought Cooper both a marriage (that lasted 40 years) and a near-fatal heart attack. Similarly, while O'Brien was deeply involved in what he felt was a compromised special effects schedule, his unstable wife shot and killed their two sons and attempted to take her own life, but survived. The shell-shocked O'Brien, already unhappy with the movie's comedic tone, finished his work, but requested his name be removed, which Cooper did not grant.

The Son of Kong - as movie and as history - is a tale of high fantasy and brutal reality, of major success rewarded by a rushed, penny-pinching struggle to meet a Christmas deadline. It is the A to Z of painful heartbreak and glorious craft rolled into nine difficult months that gave birth to 69 pleasant minutes, which we are still writing about 90 years later. In other words, just another year in the life of Hollywood.

1940

STEVEN PEROS

After 18 years working on stage and screen in his native Hungary, 38-year-old Bela Lugosi came to New Orleans in 1920 as a crewman on a merchant ship. He made his way up the coast to New York, improving his English, and finding success seven years later on Broadway in a stage adaptation of Bram Stoker's *Dracula* that had been a smash in London. After 261 performances, the Broadway hit went on the road, which brought Lugosi to California, where he remained. He wasn't Universal's first or fifth choice for the role of the Vampire Count, but director Tod Browning, who had directed several of the late, great silent star Lon Chaney's finest and freakiest films, chose Lugosi. And so, when *Dracula* was released in early 1931, it was a smash hit, catapulting the 48-year-old actor to stardom.

So how, a mere nine years later, did Bela Lugosi wind up in this low budget indie shocker about a mad scientist who works for a perfume company, exacting his revenge on the family dynasty with the aid of scientifically enlarged monster bats? *The Devil Bat* was a product of

"Poverty Row" — a group of very low budget studios, so named for being on the same stretch along Gower Street in Hollywood, that all made movies on the cheap, usually in six to ten days and never for over $100,000 (usually much lower). The two companies who duked it out for dominion in the arena of low budget horror were Monogram and PRC (Producers Releasing Corporation), which produced *The Devil Bat*. Of the two, PRC seemed to make their movies with a bit more enthusiasm and creative flair, utilizing directors who tried just a tad harder than those at Monogram (where Lugosi would make *The Ape Man* and *Spooks Run Wild*, among nine other titles). This one was directed by Arkansas-born Jean Yarbrough (billed here as "Yarborough"), only his second feature after directing many musical shorts, which were popular in the 1930's. Soon after, Yarbrough would be very busy under contract at Universal Pictures where he directed four successful Abbott & Costello comedies, including *The Naughty Nineties*, which many believe has the best film record of the duo's famous "Who's on First?" routine.

But what of Lugosi and his swift journey from super-stardom to poverty row? After *Dracula*, Lugosi was poised to be Universal's great new star of this genre recently christened "horror films". Next up, Lugosi was to star in an adaptation of Mary Shelley's *Frankenstein* under the direction of Robert Florey. In the script being developed, the monster was just that — a monster, cruel and remorseless. Lugosi was not pleased with the non-speaking role, but despite popular legend, he did not "turn down the role of the Monster". Instead, a new - and very successful - director named James Whale was brought in who had a very different concept of a more sympathetic "monster". He was not keen on Lugosi in the role and by all accounts, Lugosi was happy to be dismissed from the project.

My assessment is that what happened next in Lugosi's career was a one-two punch. Punch One: Frankenstein was an enormous hit and put Boris Karloff on the map as Universal's new horror star, unburdened by what many at the studio may have felt limiting about Lugosi: his thick Hungarian accent. Punch Two: director Florey and Lugosi made a different film for Universal, *Murders in the Rue Morgue*, released in 1932, just months after *Frankenstein*, a very dark and perverse Edgar Allan Poe-based horror film (likely too dark for audiences) which has aged very well, but which was such a box office disappointment that Lugosi would never star in another Universal horror film. His highest post-*Dracula* credit at Universal in the 1930's was second billing to Karloff in four films that range from classic (1934's *The Black Cat*) to just a whole lot of fun (1935's *The Raven*). And so, nearly 60, Lugosi was now a journeyman actor, following the money wherever it led him. And at PRC and Monogram, he was "second billing" to no one. He was The Star.

In *The Devil Bat*'s opening title card, we are told that "All Heathville loved Paul Carruthers, their kindly village doctor" but that no one suspected that in his home laboratory he "found time to conduct certain private experiments — weird, terrifying experiments." Dr. Carruthers likes bats and has found a way to enlarge them via electrodes into thick monstrous flying beasts with five -foot wingspans. Clearly, he has plans for these monster bats, which crystalize when the family-owned Heath Cosmetics gives Carruthers a bonus check for $5,000 as a token of their appreciation. Carruthers smiles on the outside, but inside, he hates the Heaths, who bought Carruthers' cosmetics company from him years ago for $10,000 and turned it into millions. They had offered Carruthers stock in the company, but he preferred the cash. And now, he bristles as he watches them all become millionaires. Carruthers creates a cologne akin to "bat-nip" which he offers to key figureheads in the Heath family.

"Put it on the tender part of your neck," he tells them.

One by one, as each of them bid Carruthers goodnight, he looks at them sadly and says with finality, "Güd-Bye," knowing that before the night is over, he will have released his devil bat into the night sky, on a direct path to its victims' throats. It's one of the delights of the movie how much Lugosi performs the hell out that one word, five times throughout the movie.

After two Heath dynasty members die mysteriously on the grounds of the mansion, with two marks on their throats, Police Chief Wilkins (Hal Price) is flummoxed as to who could be responsible. Enter crack big city reporter Johnny Layton (Dave O'Brien) who comes to town with his photographer, "One-Shot" McGuire (Donald Kerr), a nickname that does not prove accurate. As two murders turn into three, the Chief just scratches his head while Reporter Johnny inexplicably becomes the de facto detective on the case. Even when it's clear that all the victims have the same perfume scent, a scent which is identified as having been manufactured by Carruthers, Chief Wilkins still thinks Johnny is off his rocker for suggesting that beloved Doc Carruthers could be responsible. When Johnny tells the Chief that Carruthers may be getting revenge for his bum business deal, the Chief still insists that Johnny is just imagining things. Clearly, this Chief needs a devil bat to fall on his head in order to suspect Carruthers of murder. Five devil bat murders later (plus a failed attempt on Johnny and "One-Shot"), Johnny traps Carruthers and splashes the killer cologne in the doc's panicked face. When the scent-crazy devil bat flies to the scene, it claims the fleeing doc as its final victim before being gunned down by Johnny.

Plot holes be damned, I love the nuttiness of this movie, beginning with its logline: a mad perfume maker pairs a deadly scent with a giant bat of his own creation in an attempt to get revenge on the family that made millions off his cosmetics company. The cheap bat effects are actually effective and dynamic, with each nosedive attack featuring a creepy elongated *"RAAAAAAHHHHH!"* bat scream. But chief of its assets is undoubtedly Bela Lugosi. When he exclaims, "Imbecile! Bombastic ignoramus!" or explains to one of the rich folk, "Your brain is too feeble to conceive what I have accomplished in the realm of science!" you can't help but swoon over his delivery of B-Movie poetry. Every time Lugosi mournfully says "Güd-Bye" to his intended victim, he only ensures that I will be saying hello to a next viewing of *The Devil Bat* in the not-too-distant future.

The Thief of Bagdad

1940

JUSTIN HUMPHREYS

The Thief of Bagdad is my favorite Arabian Nights movie. (I won't even try to suggest a "best" picture in that sub-genre—that's an exercise in futility.) It's also one of my favorite fantasy films, and there are plenty of others who feel likewise, including its staunch devotees, Francis Ford Coppola and Martin Scorsese.

The Thief of Bagdad is a loose remake of the eponymous 1924 Douglas Fairbanks silent film; the operative word being "loose". Shot in gorgeous Technicolor at England's Denham Studios, it takes a more kid-friendly approach to its material than the Fairbanks version. That's not a criticism; among its many virtues, the 1940 *Thief of Bagdad* is a great movie about being a child, and it's perceptively attuned to a kids'-eye-view of the world. Its boy hero, Abu (Sabu), gets to have all the adventures youngsters dream of going on: he outwits a gigantic djinn and gets three wishes, battles a giant spider, and flies on a magic carpet, among other things. (The late actress Susan Tyrrell once told me she idolized Sabu as a little girl, and wanted to *be* him.) There's also a fabulous throwaway gag where Abu tells his friend King Ahmad that he has booked passage for them with a certain sailor: Sinbad. In a moment most kids will easily relate to, Abu's face lights up with horror at the prospect of having to go to school. Luckily, his flying carpet is standing by. The film is also a kids' primer in things that deeply matter, like courage, wit, and loyalty.

Abu is a wily trickster who, through various fanciful circumstances, winds up allied with the deposed King of Bagdad, Ahmad (John Justin).

The sinister Vizier, Jaffar (Conrad Veidt), has designs not only on ruling Bagdad, but on Ahmad's lady love, the Princess (June Duprez), so he blinds Ahmad and transforms Abu into a dog. (The film was made during World War II, so the conniving villain is notably played by a German with a pronounced accent.)

Our heroes are separated. Abu frees a menacing djinn (Rex Ingram) from his bottle and cleverly tricks him into servitude. To find his lost friend, Abu bravely steals the All-Seeing Eye, a magical jewel, from the Temple of the Dawn, which leads him to Ahmad. Jaffar recaptures Ahmad and, as he faces imminent execution, Abu saves him and kills Jaffar.

The film's trailer promised "the miracle picture of all time", and that was barely exaggeration. Its extraordinarily talented creative team included co-directors Ludwig Berger and Michael Powell, before he reinvented cinematic storytelling with masterpieces like *Black Narcissus* (1947) and *The Red Shoes* (1948). Members of the special effects team, Lawrence Butler and Jack Whitney, won an Academy Award for their work, and cinematographer Georges Perinal won for Best Cinematography. *The Thief of Bagdad* abounds with wonders — among them, the djinn, a flying clockwork horse, and the Silver Maid, a six-armed, guitar-playing automaton that kills the dithering Sultan (the hilarious Miles Malleson, who also cowrote the script).

But the topic at hand is giant beasts, and *The Thief of Bagdad* has both the gargantuan djinn (who I *guess* counts because most genies — including one in this book — are depicted as human-sized) and a giant spider Abu must defeat to reach the All-Seeing Eye. This shaggy horror is central to this bravura sequence — a reworking of a scene from the Fairbanks film — and arguably *The Thief of Bagdad*'s creative apex.

To steal the jewel and locate Ahmad, Abu travels on the djinn's back to the Temple of the Dawn, and his voyage to and through it is a masterclass in fantasy filmmaking. The imaginative powerhouse behind it was William Cameron Menzies, for whom the term "Production Designer" was originally coined, based on his inestimable contributions to *Gone with the Wind*. A moviemaking visionary of the highest order, Menzies' many notable works include designing the 1924 *Thief of Bagdad*, and designing and directing *Things to Come* (1936, also shot at Denham) and *Invaders from Mars* (1953). Menzies was hired by producer Alexander Korda mainly to oversee and direct the effects-heavy scenes between Sabu and Ingram, and his gifted eye—no pun intended —is intensely apparent in every square inch of the Temple of the Dawn.

The giant spider here is only one facet of the gem that is the sequence as a whole. One striking image after another, all masterfully composed and color-coordinated, builds up to Abu first battling the spider, then stealing the All-Seeing Eye. *The Thief of Bagdad*'s Oscar-winning special effects marked a quantum leap in the use of blue-backing traveling mattes. It's F/X-laden throughout. Miniatures, matte paintings, and matte shots were all used for the temple, which accounts for the blue halos around its green guardians, seen scurrying around and seemingly dwarfed by what is, in fact, a miniature.

The trip to the Temple of Dawn is bookended by the djinn's hyperbolic pronouncements. The temple, he explains, is located "On the highest peak of the highest mountain of the world, where earth meets the sky… and in the Great Hall of the Temple is the Goddess of Light, and in the head of the goddess is the All-Seeing Eye!" But between the djinn's bursts of bluster, this segment is nearly dialogue-free, except for Abu singing his signature song, which echoes through the vast temple. Miklos Rozsa's excellent score beautifully punctuates key moments. As the djinn drops Abu off, he tells him "And, now, my little braggart, you can be a thief and a hero all in one!" In this case, the loyal Abu's thievery will ultimately save Ahmad.

Obviously nervous, Abu perseveres, making his way through the temple with its ornate Indian statuary, to its central, moodily-lit, many-armed Goddess of Light statue. The armored, armed skeletons littering the idol's inner entrance show Abu and the audience that something awful guards it. (The neatly organized rows of skulls in the background are a marvelous touch.) Taking a sword from a skeleton's hand to defend himself with, Abu discovers the spider's sprawling web, spun among swirling, sinuous designs in the walls, high over a pool where an octopus lurks.

When Abu faces the spider, it's initially a puppet, and a surprisingly effective one. Some of these shots were done at General Service Studios in Hollywood, rather than Denham. Its unnatural movements give it an otherworldly quality that's only partly undercut when it moves into brighter light, revealing it to be an obvious model. Shots of full-size legs swinging at Abu work well, and it would surprise no one if this encounter partly inspired the confrontation between Scott Carey, the tiny hero of 1957's *The Incredible Shrinking Man*, and a massive arachnid.

As Abu and the spider swing at each other, he slashes the strand of web it dangles from, sending it plummeting down into the pool. Then, the scene builds to its aesthetically stunning and awe-inspiring climax: the theft of the All-Seeing Eye. The use of complementary colors on the enormous statue is visually stunning: the pale blue of the figure and its countless arms, offset by the green of its eyes and mouth and the glowing red of the jewel.

Although the spider is a pivotal part of the scene, it seems almost anticlimactic alongside the visual splendor and sheer scope of the idol. Sometimes, even a giant monster is no match for a gifted art director. Usually, it's the giant monster that swallows things whole, but Menzies' magnificent art direction devours this particular creature alive.

The Thief of Bagdad looks and feels like a gorgeously-illustrated storybook sprung to life. It was costly in its day, and every penny spent on it is up there onscreen. Without being precious or sappy, it exquisitely captures on film — more than any other movie before or since — the essence of a fairytale.

1949

LARRY BLAMIRE

Since the title contains two of my favorite words, it was inevitable that I like this movie. But let's cut right to the elephant in the room, and by elephant of course, I mean dinosaur, and by dinosaur, I mean men-in-suits, and by men-in-suits, I mean men-in-suits-who-have-trouble-moving. Will that keep Larry from enjoying this movie?

My dinosaur needs are simple: people run around in a jungle and get eaten by dinosaurs. Which is why I think *Jurassic Park III* is the best of that series. *Unknown Island,* directed by Jack Bernhard, written by Robert T. Shannon and Jack Harvey, is the only dinosaur movie of the 1940's (with the exception of 1940's *One Million B.C.,* which wasn't set in the present day). There wouldn't be another until *Lost Continent* three years later, and my favorite of that decade would have to be Universal's *The Land Unknown* (1957). I confess I somehow did not see *Unknown Island* as a kid, and only stumbled onto the dinosaur scenes late one night as an adult, convinced I was hallucinating (they are pretty strange out of context).

Unknown Island's opening titles are over a pleasing still of the matte shot of the island seen later when the characters first arrive, and the Cinecolor (the old two-color process) makes it look both quaint and adventurous. The opening scene in a seedy dockside dive is, like much of the film, pure pulp. In Singapore, Ted Osborne (Philip Reed) and fiancée Carole Lane (feisty Virginia Grey) charter a tramp steamer operated by roughneck Captain Tarnowski (Barton MacLane), First Mate Sanderson (Dick Wessel) and crewman Edwards (future *Attack of the Giant Leeches* victim Dan White), to take them to an uncharted island of living dinosaurs (spotted by Osborne in a WWII flyover), so that he can photograph them and be rich and famous. To assist them, they shanghai drunken-wretch dino-survivor John Fairbanks (Richard Denning).

I will say without further ado that Barton MacLane's Captain Tarnowski is the roaring freight train that barrels this movie along. Drinking, bellowing, laughing abrasively at the discomfort of others, he is instantly lovable. Within minutes, he pitches a guy through a doorway just to make room. Even before he meets Carole he's already planning his conquest of her, his brash confidence betraying a stunning lack of self-awareness. He leers at her right in front of her betrothed, who's finagling to hire the captain's ship. Sanderson is his best friend and even *he* hates him (the most unhinged moment comes later when Tarnowski sneaks up on the latter in the jungle camp, grabs him with a fire tool, screams, then laughs at his distress). Whatever MacLane might have thought of this project, it doesn't show, as he gives it his professional all to make sure it's entertaining. The character's arrogant belligerence will not subside until his untimely encounter with a carnivorous, giant sloth.

It's fun to see Richard Denning, stalwart 1950's monster-battler of *The Creature from the Black Lagoon* (1954), *The Day the World Ended* (1955) and *The Black Scorpion* (1957), as a shabby tortured soul, drowning his trauma in whiskey after seeing his buddies eaten by dinosaurs. Virginia Grey (looking great in jodhpurs), with a Hollywood career that would span six decades, gives a gritty all-in performance as Carole. These two would work together again in the robot invasion film, *Target Earth* (1954).

After humiliating the drunken Fairbanks (because he can), Tarnowski agrees to the expedition, despite the fact that Osborne's single photographic proof of his wild dinosaur claim looks somewhat like a children's book illustration. As we know from *King Kong*, nothing says adventure like an old tramp steamer (this is not the only similarity to that RKO classic, making it a sort of minor reimagining), unglamorously-named the Pelican, described by Tarnowski and Sanderson as a "floating pigpen."

Before you know it, Fairbanks cleans up from pathetic wretch ("too much sun has scrambled his brains") to reluctant hero and begins a flinty relationship with Carole that grows to infatuation. Her fiancée's obsession (let's call it "Carl Denham Fever") with dinosaur photography will fester into classic career-over-family dysfunction, and when Virginia Grey stands at the railing looking out to sea, we can't help but think of Fay Wray's Ann Darrow. The more Osborne ignores her, the less Fairbanks does, and we are reminded that, of course, Ann Darrow ended up with Jack Driscoll. As the journey progresses, the crew air their superstitions about being this far off the Borneo route, speaking in hushed tones of the "taboo island rising out of the sea." This leads to a botched mutiny, which is relegated to a brief montage, with an annoyingly superimposed clock (passage of time) to shorthand it.

Once on the island, Fairbanks, still monster-shy, indicates they're probably safer by the shore. "They won't come to you, with the exception of that hairy monster I was telling you about. He'll look *us* up." Well, actually, we're a half-hour in and this is the first we're hearing of what is the film's Kong surrogate, the giant sloth. The first dinosaurs we see are Brontosauruses, on a ridge, then in a shallow pond, and they look pretty good, particularly when one moves through the water. The next ones up are Dimetrodons (technically not dinosaurs), and these are even more impressive as the legs are motorized, which, in conjunction with a cable to pull them along, looks reasonably convincing. The only drawbacks are the immobile eyes, a feature shared by the next ones encountered, the theropods. These (apparently Ceratosauruses) end up being the least convincing, probably because they were the most challenging for a movie on this type of budget. They look good, they just don't move well, and it stems from the fact that these were in fact very large suits, as Bob Burns would attest (more on that later).

The sight of no less than five of these big-suited beasts wobbling about a field of bones is decidedly odd. Tarnowski remarks, "Looks like a prehistoric graveyard" but I thought it looked more like a dinosaur shopping mall. I have to say, one thing that helps sell the dinosaur encounters is the sheer intensity of the "victim-screams". We're talking some shrill and desperate screeches from hapless crewmen (think: *King Kong*), such as the poor guy lying in the desert, bookended by matching Ceratosauruses.

Earlier, when Fairbanks finally agreed to go ashore, he sneered at Tarnowski, "I wanna hear you when you start screaming." Thanks to the giant sloth, he gets his wish. We last see Tarnowski in closeup, screaming like a baby, as Fairbanks and Carole return to the ship, and a surprisingly understanding Osborne, who graciously concedes to the better man.

As the amazing Bob Burns (custodian supreme of remarkable props and the original Monster Kid) related to Tom Weaver in his indispensable *Monster Kid Memories*, at age 13, he was fortunate enough to befriend prop master Ellis Burman (via his son) and not only behold the dinosaur suits in person, but to be on location in Palmdale for the shooting of the scenes in (what the movie refers to as) the island's "flat, barren area" (read: desert). The therapod suits were enormous for man-in-suit work (eight or nine feet high), and the extras inside suffered in 100 degree heat. Bob could attest to the quality of Burman's craftsmanship when he first saw the constructs in the workshop, and they looked pretty impressive out there in the desert, too. But he noted that, in seeing the film, they were not quite as successful because of those limitations of movement. The poor guys inside did what they could. But Bob added that he still liked them just the same. And so do I.

1949

JUSTIN HUMPHREYS

Mighty Joe Young has been written about at such length for so many decades that it's nearly impossible to come up with anything new to say about its production. Willis O'Brien and Ray Harryhausen, the towering creative talents who brought its titular gorilla to life, have been the subjects of endless articles and books—at last count, I think there were about 8,000 books on Harryhausen alone. And rightly so: despite the fact they were pioneering stop-motion animation "by gosh and by guess," as renowned *Famous Monsters of Filmland* editor, Forrest J. Ackerman, would say, they showed enormous quality and skill, and there's a genuine vision at work in their films. This is all to say that this essay won't just rehash behind-the-scenes details on their virtuoso animation; it's more of an appreciation of the film and its good-natured spirit.

At the risk of stating the obvious, *Mighty Joe Young* is a semi-remake of 1933's *King Kong*, wrought by key members of *Kong*'s creative team: producer Merian C. Cooper (who also concocted the original story), director Ernest Schoedsack, screenwriter Ruth Rose, and stop-motion wizard Willis O'Brien. Cooper produced the film independently under the aegis of Argosy Pictures, his company with John Ford, and

Ford regulars Ben Johnson and Jack Pennick both memorably appear in it. The overriding, overall difference between *Mighty Joe Young* and *King Kong* is in tone, partly due to when they were respectively made: *King Kong* is shot through with an edge of Depression-Era harshness (tempered by some Ruby Keeler-like overnight-sensation pipe dreams), whereas *Mighty Joe Young*, released in 1949, is suffused with post-War optimism. *Mighty Joe Young* is a soft-hearted animal-lover's movie, and it subversively makes its gorilla hero infinitely more sympathetic and human than most of the human characters.

Monster movies frequently tend to sympathize with their creatures, particularly natural beasts like Joe Young who are just minding their own business. It's human interlopers encroaching on the putative monsters' territory that stirs up trouble in the first place, usually followed by the monsters' tragic undoing. Look no further than *King Kong, Creature from the Black Lagoon, Gorgo, The Abominable Snowman of the Himalayas*, ad infinitum. Just like in real life, human beings have little or no sense of when to leave well enough alone, and their screwing around with nature usually sours everything, which could mean a flattened city or, at minimum, a trail of corpses. Even when monsters pack a brutal edge, like Kong or the Gill-man, the audience is in solidarity with them: they are being set upon and are simply defending themselves.

This undertone was a key reason why *King Kong* struck such a nerve. Kong is an unfortunate victim of exploitative human beings, and he's not alone. Notably, when adventurer/filmmaker Carl Denham's men first encounter a Stegosaurus on Skull Island in the film, they barely try to bypass it and, when it charges, they kill it. If its species wasn't already extinct, they pretty well finished the job.

Mighty Joe Young hits most of the same plot points as *King Kong*, but far more gently. It begins in Africa, where a little girl, Jill Young, adopts a baby gorilla, and names him Joe. In a very perceptive piece of dialogue, her father firmly tells her: "I will not raise a gorilla." Dissolve to him watching Joe drink from his bottle, and warmly remarking "How the little fellow loves his milk." How many real dads have said something like that nearly verbatim about the cat or dog their kid brought home that they inadvertently fell for?

Twelve years later, fast-talking New York promoter/pitchman Max

O'Hara (Carl Denham himself, Robert Armstrong) travels to Africa to capture wildlife for his new Hollywood nightspot, the Golden Safari. He and his cowboys inadvertently stumble onto the full-grown Joe, now much larger than an average gorilla (but, notably, still less intimidatingly huge than Kong). After a fracas between Joe and O'Hara's men, teenage Jill (Terry Moore) calms Joe down and we see how gentle and obedient he is with her. They're trespassing on her land, and she's not having it: "You keep off him, you big bullies!" she hollers. Unlike Kong, Joe isn't a wild beast: he's a domesticated pet.

Jill befriends one of O'Hara's men, champion roper Gregg Johnson (real-life champion roper Ben Johnson, as natural on-camera as ever), and he starts looking out for the naïve, unworldly girl. With the promise of glitz and fame, O'Hara convinces Jill to bring Joe to Hollywood to headline at his new nightclub, the Golden Safari. As in *King Kong*, when presented with an awe-inspiring natural marvel like Joe — the 9th Wonder of the World, if you will — any sense of respect for the creature's nobility vanishes and the big guy winds up appearing in a tacky stage show for the amusement of a stupid, drunken audience.

Seeing Joe depressed in his cage, Jill speaks for the audience when she exclaims "My poor Joe!" In an idiotic organ-grinder's monkey act, the crowd pelts Joe with oversize coins, infuriating him. Later, some loutish drunks give Joe booze and abuse him, and he goes on a rampage, wrecking the Golden Safari. As the movie's trailer bellowed: "See Mighty Joe Young, enraged by Hollywood pranksters, destroy filmland's swankiest nightclubs on the fabulous Sunset Strip!"

Joe is captured and is going to be shot. In a change of heart, O'Hara masterminds an escape plan to get Joe back to Africa and helps Jill and Gregg abscond with him. During a breakneck chase with the police, they happen upon a burning orphanage — as you do — and stop to help evacuate the kids. Joe braves the flames, saves a little girl, and becomes a hero. In the epilogue, Jill and Gregg send O'Hara a home movie of them and Joe waving from her African ranch. "They're back home, where they belong," O'Hara says. The end card warmly tells us: "Goodbye from Joe Young."

Throughout the film, what really sells Joe as not merely an animated puppet but as a flesh-and-blood character is the personality that Harryhausen, working from Willis O'Brien's layouts, so beautifully imbues him with. Although those are just dolls' eyes rolling around in Joe's sockets, Harryhausen gives them a very real animality: Joe's expressions of fright, sadness, and rage register marvelously. It's a full-bodied performance, and the improvements in puppet-making and animation since *King Kong* are vividly there onscreen, particularly in Joe's fur, which remains smooth throughout the stop-motion process, without the heavy "chatter" of the Kong puppets' rabbit fur.

One of my fondest memories of *Mighty Joe Young* is having cataloged a collection of behind-the-scenes photos that once belonged to Orville Beckett, one of O'Brien's ongoing technicians. The pictures clearly conveyed the production's atmosphere: gag shots of Joe Young with a Santa beard perched by the chimney of a snowy house; puppets posed mock-threateningly, about to jokingly attack their creators; Joe Young puppets in a dance line; etc. The whimsy onscreen was obviously contagious.

In *Mighty Joe Young*, it's fascinating watching how antiquated popular misconceptions about gorillas were beginning to fade. Myths about them being fearsome, terrifying monsters — which had been promulgated by things like Ringling Brothers' ballyhoo of their gorilla, Gargantua — were giving way to the knowledge that they are essentially mild creatures. There's a sense of love and respect for animals in *Mighty Joe Young* that's vaguely reminiscent of, say, Roald Dahl's moving short story "The Boy Who Talked with Animals". *Mighty Joe Young* is sweet without being cloying, and, although it's definitely not subtle, it winningly makes its points about the monstrousness of man and the humaneness of monsters.

THE SNOW CREATURE

1954

MIKE PEROS

When I selected *The Snow Creature* from the list of monster movies I could write about, I had based this on fond memories of having seen this film in my youth. Content with my choice, I sat on my living room couch, turned the film on (off a YouTube print), and about five minutes in, I felt like Spencer Tracy in *Guess Who's Coming to Dinner* after he samples an eagerly anticipated scoop of Oregon Boysenberry ice cream and mutters, "This is not the stuff." As it turns out, I must have mistaken this *Snow Creature* for any number of subsequent films containing a snow monster of some kind. (It might well be *Abominable Snowman of the Himalayas* but some other lucky scribe will be writing about that in a later chapter.)

As for my *Snow Creature*, something that may surprise viewers is that it was directed by Billy Wilder's older brother, Wilhelm Wilder, who went by the professional name of W. Lee Wilder, perhaps to avoid confusion with his younger, more established brother. Wilder had worked in retail, but spurred on (I hesitate to say, encouraged) by his brother's success, he moved from Long Island to Hollywood to get a foothold in the film industry. One of Wilder's earliest efforts was as the producer of director Anthony Mann's *The Great Flamarion* (1946) starring Erich von Stroheim, who had been in Billy Wilder's *Five Graves to Cairo* (1943), and Dan Duryea (the subject of my first biography, *Dan Duryea: Heel with a Heart*), here playing an alcoholic weakling. Wilder found his niche directing low-budget genre films, including another 1946 noir *The Glass Alibi* (its plot concerning two lovers plotting to rid themselves of an unwanted spouse, reminiscent of Billy Wilder's 1944 classic, *Double Indemnity*), the sci-fi *Phantom from Space* (1953), and the relatively prestigious *Bluebeard's Ten Honeymoons* (1960) starring George Sanders opposite a bevy of soon-to-be slain beauties.

However, W. Lee was not the only Wilder associated with *The Snow Creature* — the screenplay is by W. Lee's son, Myles, who wrote scripts for a number of his father's movies, including the aforementioned *Phantom from Space* and *Bluebeard's Ten Honeymoons*, *Manfish*, and *Spy in the Sky*. Myles would also segue to a successful and lengthy career in television, writing for such hits as *Bonanza*, *My Three Sons*, *Get Smart*, *Welcome Back Kotter*, and *The Dukes of Hazzard*.

The Snow Creature was the first film to take the myth of the Yeti and turn it into a sci-fi/horror film. After some portentous opening narration and a brief credit sequence, we are plunged into the snowy Himalayas. The film's narrator/protagonist is leading botanist Doctor Frank Parrish, played by Paul Langton, who would find fame as Leslie Harrington on television's *Peyton Place*. Parrish, along with cynical photographer Peter Wells (Leslie Denison) and a small group of Sherpas led by the English-speaking Subra (Teru Shimada) are heading into the Himalayas for unspecified botanical pursuits. Subra shares a tender moment with his wife before he begins the trek — if you have your foreshadowing shoes on, you know what this means. This section is slow, but how can you hate a movie where the narrator alerts us to this: "The first days were uneventful, monotonous, tedious."

We do spend some time with the main characters as they're huddled in their tents. Photographer Wells does what "movie photographers" normally do: he drinks his Scotch right out of the bottle. It's clear that botany is important to Parrish when he chooses to persist with his botanical pursuits even after the Snow Creature carries off Subra's "woman". When Subra wants to track and kill the creature, Parrish dresses him down. (The narration tends to be overstated here: "Because of my decision, I felt Subra resented and disliked me.") Subra then steals Parrish's gun and rallies the other Sherpas to curtail the expedition and instead hunt for the Yeti. The wily Subra also shoots their concealed short-wave radio and grabs all the Scotch (this last development horrifies Wells).

About this Snow Creature: One hopes the creature might have been at least a little… terrifying. Quite often, though, it appears to be someone clad in an Eskimo jacket with some mud caked on him, being directed to glower. It's not especially convincing, and because the Snow Creature is shot either under cover of darkness or obscured by snow, it's none too frightening.

Meanwhile, the Snow Creature appears that night to kill a Sherpa, then precipitates a deadly avalanche, and yet, botanist Parrish hints that Subra could be famous if they bring the Yeti in *alive*.

A few things to note here: One is Parrish's obvious unfamiliarity with *King Kong* (discussed in our first chapter); another is the lengths to which Parrish will go in order to manipulate Subra. (Subra is unmoved by Parrish's entreaties: "Subra kill all Yeti."). Wells says to Parrish: "Move over, Macduff," a Shakespeare allusion that is striking for its incongruity.

In short order, the men find a cave with Subra's woman's necklace, then find the Snow Creature and its own woman, along with a baby Yeti. The cave collapses, killing the woman and baby while stunning the Snow Creature. Parrish grabs the gun from Subra, gives the unconscious Yeti an injection, and insists that Subra and the Sherpas carry the creature down the mountain. In the village, an obliging official accedes to Parrish's request to transport the subdued Yeti back to the States in a frozen crate.

Back in the USA (Los Angeles International Airport), we briefly meet Parrish's wife before she then disappears from the film. The Snow Creature is still in the box, but in the film's only offbeat development, it is detained at Customs while Parrish and Immigration wrangle over who/what the creature is, especially since photographer Wells has published an article portraying the creature as a "Snow Man." While its/his status is being debated, the creature escapes, clobbers a guard, and kills a young woman. Since it's responsible for at least two deaths already, it isn't surprising that Police Lieutenant Dunbar (William Phipps) wants the creature dead, yet botanist Parrish insists that it be "stopped, not killed."

Given the nocturnal hunt for the homicidal Snow Creature, the movie starts to resemble Anthony Mann's classic 1949 noir, *He Walked by Night*, what with the creature finding shelter (in this case, a meat-packing facility, where it ostensibly feels at home among the frozen carcasses), the pursuers' puzzlement at how the Creature can elude their dragnet, and the realization that it might be moving through storm drains. Though the creature appears often, any tension is dissipated by repetitive close-ups of it approaching the camera. The police place a net around the flailing yeti, and Lt. Dunbar shoots it dead (immigration status unresolved). All pursuers, even Parrish, are in good spirits, more so when Dunbar is told that there is a "creature" waiting for him at home. This comes courtesy of his previously expectant wife and provides a note of levity as the film concludes, and the lengthy credits roll.

As a forerunner of other "Abominable Snowman" films, *The Snow Creature* is almost without merit, though the fact that the low budget meant keeping the creature "in the shadows" probably helps more than hurts. The parts that spark the most interest are the exchanges over the creature's humanity; all else is unrelieved mediocrity. And while the photographer character, Wells, has potential, he is given short shrift by screenwriter Myles Wilder. (Though Wilder would later write for a slew of successful sitcoms, there is little evidence of that wit here.) At least the monster comes in and starts killing early, but in the end, *The Snow Creature* is a missed opportunity; later films would more effectively explore the myth of the Yeti. And yet even with these criticisms, I dare say, *The Snow Creature* is necessary viewing for the die-hard Yeti Cinema completist. Just don't say I didn't warn you.

IT CAME FROM BENEATH THE SEA

1955

MIKE PEROS

In the early 1990's, I began attending the San Diego Comic-Con when it was still in its infancy. At first, I was there to play a character called Tromie the Nuclear Rodent, which had been the brainchild of Lloyd Kaufman of Troma Films. It was a terrific experience, wherein I got to be on a panel (as Tromie) and also meet the great Adam West (who looked at me in my Tromie outfit and proclaimed me the most repulsive thing he had ever seen). There was a certain energy in those early days of the con, before it was overtaken by the major studios and before the advent of anime and manga. One of the things I enjoyed most was attending panels. There were lines of course, but nothing like now. You never knew who you might see, such as bumping into *Star Trek*'s Chekhov (Walter Koenig) near the conference rooms, or, along with my brother Steve, helping *The* (true) *Avengers*' John Steed, aka Patrick Macnee, find the way to his own convention appearance.

One particularly fond memory was attending the annual joint appearances of stop-motion pioneer Ray Harryhausen, author Ray Bradbury, and *Famous Monsters of Filmland* titan Forrest J. Ackerman. The three would hold court in one of the conference rooms at the Convention Center; sometimes it would be just Harryhausen and Bradbury in a program called "A Couple of Rays." These were always lively talks which not only provided insights into their personal lives, but also into their professional war stories: the inspiration behind some of Bradbury's cautionary tales or the nuts and bolts of how Harryhausen created his effects for his sci-fi/fantasy classics from the 1950's through the early 1980's. There was plenty of love in these rooms, from the fans who were present, and from Harryhausen, Bradbury, and Ackerman themselves, how proud they were of their work and how happy they were that it has endured. After their chats, you could amble up to them and sneak in a moment of praise or small talk, and they were unfailingly gracious and happy to meet *you*.

Seeing these creative giants led me to revisit their work, so I was thrilled that Ray Harryhausen's 1955 classic, *It Came from Beneath the Sea*, was included in this volume. I remembered the film as being effective, especially when the monster (in this case, a giant octopus) made its appearances, but it's also of interest for other reasons. The film was made at Columbia under the aegis of Sam Katzman, who ran a "B" unit there, and though Charles Schneer was the producer of record, and Robert Gordon is credited as director, the Katzman touch is present, meaning if a cost needed to be cut, Katzman was the man to do it. Which is why you might only see six tentacles on the film's giant octopus, as Katzman wouldn't give Harryhausen the funding to animate the other two.

One common thread in these 1950's monster films is the growing threat of radioactivity on nature. *It Came from Beneath* the Sea begins with a nuclear submarine getting entangled with some massive being — and after extricating itself, the crew finds some rubbery tissue stuck in its gears. Kenneth Tobey, who had led the expedition in 1951's *The Thing* is on board as Commander Pete Matthews, captain of the submarine. Tobey hopes that "it's the end of it," but the portentous narrator lets us know it's not the end, but a problem "beyond the scope of Navy men."

This means the Navy must bring in the marine biologists, namely Professors Lesley Joyce and John Carter and (played by Faith Domergue and Donald Curtis), and it's the relationship among Tobey, Domergue, and Curtis that is refreshingly adult for its time. Domergue had scored a recent hit with 1955's *This Island Earth* and had earlier impressed as the femme fatale in 1950's *Where Danger Lives*. By this point, Domergue's characters exhibited a blend of intelligence, pragmatism, and vulnerability. She ignores Tobey's request that she be replaced with "someone different" (as in, a man); while she is studying the mysterious tissue, Tobey comes on strong, but Domergue puts him in his place: "Your objectives are not necessarily my own." After twelve days of intensive examination, Captain Tobey convinces Domergue's professor to take a break. He is also curious about her friend, Professor Curtis — he's a little older, they seem mighty close, but how close are they? The film plays coy with this for a while, but we know who gets top billing. On the thirteenth day, the professors find out definitively that the tissue belongs to a giant octopus that had been disturbed by the hydrogen bomb. Since they've done what the Navy has asked, the two professors plan to go to Egypt to mix business with some pleasure.

We soon learn their work is not finished, since the same giant octopus proceeds to wreak havoc on a tramp steamer, abandoning its seafood diet to enjoy some human tidbits. At the same time, Captain Tobey is melting Domergue's defenses by treating Domergue and Curtis to lobster (as opposed to a manly T-bone). After some passionate embraces, Tobey presumes Domergue will abandon her Egypt plans, but no, she's resolute — at least until they hear of the attack on the steamer. None of the few survivors will admit to the monstrous nature of the attack for fear of being institutionalized, but Domergue, using feminine wiles and every gentle, persuasive weapon in her arsenal, elicits from one survivor that it was indeed a giant octopus that destroyed the vessel.

The Egypt trip is postponed, as Tobey and Domergue head to Harper's Cove on a hunch that the monster may be there, though the deputy there is none too sure. There are giant prints in the sand, so their hunch may be correct. As they wait, the two new colleagues fish, swim, and continue to get closer. Tobey then tries to pull rank and convince Domergue to leave the monster-hunting to the men, but she insists on staying, just as the octopus makes its way to shore and kills the heretofore skeptical deputy.

Luckily, Tobey and Domergue are able to gather their beach gear and return to San Francisco, where the octopus is laying waste to San Francisco's infrastructure, namely a section of the Golden Gate Bridge, which necessitates a dramatic rescue of Professor Curtis by Captain Tobey. The octopus then makes its way inland, with its giant tentacles showing no mercy as they damage buildings and crush unlucky citizens. This monster's rampage is pretty effective in its integration of stop-motion special effects, miniatures, and a large model tentacle. What also works here dramatically is the teamwork involved in bringing down this monster, from the use of flame throwers to drive it offshore to Commander Tobey taking out the sub and using a torpedo to finish the job (which necessitates *him* now being rescued by Curtis).

With the mission accomplished and mankind saved, the important business of who ends up with whom needs to be decided. As before, it's Domergue's scientist/independent woman who dictates the terms. As Professor Curtis approvingly looks on, it is Domergue who tells Tobey that she's heading to Egypt and will be writing a book - with Tobey - about capturing the sea beast. Tobey can't help but go along, while remarking that Curtis may be "right about this new breed of women." It's an amusing way to end a film that is rightly celebrated for its special effects, but also deserves praise for its depiction of men/women relationships, both professional and personal. Its reminder that opinions on traditional gender roles can evolve, and that a woman needn't give up her vocation just to be with another man — even if he is tough, old-fashioned Commander Tobey.

1955/1957

BRIAN R. SOLOMON

Sometimes, the practice common to mid-20th century Hollywood of re-editing, re-mixing and otherwise re-building Japanese special effects films ("*tokusatsu*") for the American moviegoing audience actually had some pretty decent and memorable results. The most famous of all of these, of course, would be *Gojira* (1954), the Toho Studios movie that launched the Japanese giant monster ("*kaiju*") genre. That movie would be transformed into *Godzilla: King of the Monsters* (1956), and centered around Raymond Burr as the sober narrator, improbably named Steve Martin. Most would agree that the Ishiro Honda-directed movie in its original form is superior, but the Burr version has lots of fan support and is loved in its own right.

Nevertheless, this success wasn't always assured, and it certainly wasn't with *Half Human*, a movie that has one of the most obscure and circuitous backstories of any film in the Japanese *tokusatsu* canon. But despite its lackluster reputation, *Half Human*, or *Ju jin yuki otoko* as it was originally known in Japan, is a very important film in the cycle of Japanese fantasy and science fiction cinema. It came along at a time when Toho was in the process of finding itself, just before the so-called "Kaiju Boom" took place, and is a fascinating step toward the creation of a movie subgenre that continues to tickle monster movie fans two-thirds of a century later. It also happens to be a lot of fun for lovers of kitsch and mid-century sci-fi oddities.

The beginning of the journey that led to this unfairly overlooked and largely forgotten film goes all the way back to the beginning of Toho's reinvention of itself as a purveyor of tokusatsu and monster movie gems, with that aforementioned flick about the giant lizard that incinerated Tokyo. Immediately after the completion of *Gojira* but before the movie had even been released, Toho head honcho Tomoyuki Tanaka quickly greenlit the production of a different kind of monster movie, intended to capitalize on the Yeti-mania that had overtaken popular culture in the 1950's thanks to the infamous 1951 discovery of massive footprints on Mount Everest by English explorer Eric Shipton. Other early capitalizers on this craze would include the 1957 British film *The Abominable Snowman of the Himalayas* (which helped lend the creature its colloquialized name) and the American movie *The Snow Creature* (1954) before that (see chapters on both).

Author Shigeru Kayama, who had contributed the original story for *Gojira*, was brought back to come up with a new original concept that would feature a humanoid snow creature, originally given the cryptic name S-Project. *Gojira* director Honda, a journeyman who took on whatever project Toho put in front of him in those days, was also brought back to helm the new project. By the end of 1954, mere weeks after the theatrical release of *Gojira*, what was then called *Snowman of the Alps* was put into production, with a finished screenplay based on Kayama's story by *Gojira* screenwriter Takeo Murata.

The film that would be released (briefly) to Japanese cinemas starred the 21-year-old Akira Takarada, less than two years in the business and hot off the success of *Gojira*, and the similarly young newcomer Momoki Kochi, who had co-starred with him in *Gojira* as well. It told the story of a group of young skiers who are separated while on a trip to the Japanese Alps. One is killed and one goes missing, with all clues pointing to a large, mysterious creature as the culprit. Returning months later after the snow has melted, they bring with them scientist Koizumi (played by Akira Kurosawa stock player Nobuo Nakamura, known to kaiju fans for his 1960's work in *Dogora, Frankenstein Conquers the World,* and *War of the Gargantuas*) in an attempt to find their friend and prove the existence of the beast.

Unbeknownst to them, they're also being trailed by unscrupulous circus promoter Oba (30-year film veteran Yoshio Kosugi, best known to monster fans as the tribal chief in *King Kong vs. Godzilla*), who wants to exploit the creature for monetary gain, naturally. Along the way, the cast is alternately menaced and assisted by a tribe of grotesque, inbred mountain natives who worship the creature and its young offspring. Tsuburaya's design for the towering snowman, played by Sanshiro Sagawa in what was apparently his only role, is somewhat crude compared to the wonders he'd create in years to come, but the headpiece and mask design allows for a surprising amount of expressiveness, which is helpful, as we're meant to sympathize with the creature who merely wants to live his life in peace — a peace ripped apart when his offspring is killed, leading to a mad spree of destruction that levels the natives' village.

Unfortunately, the finished product *Ju jin yuki otoko* (literally translated as *Tree Person Snowman*), released in August 1955, did not last long in Japanese theaters, as it became the target of protest from native advocate groups who claimed that the savage tribesmen depicted in the movie were based on the real-life Burakumin, a native ethnic group traditionally discriminated against in Japan's historically rigid caste-based feudal system. Looking to recoup its losses, Toho decided to turn to the American market and try and duplicate what had been done with *Gojira*.

The result was the drive-in oddity *Half Human,* released in May 1957 in a completely recut and reedited version that rendered it nearly unrecognizable from the original Japanese film Honda had made. Cobbled together by Kenneth G. Crane, an editor of TV dramas and variety shows, and paired with a second Crane effort, *Monster from Green Hell* (reviewed in *Giant Bug Cinema*), on a double bill, it contained a fraction of the actual footage shot by Honda, and totally removed the musical score written by Masaru Sato. All Japanese footage was shown in flashback, with not a word of Japanese (or any other language) heard from any of the original actors.

Shoehorned into the movie were a series of wraparound scenes anchored by John Carradine, that Barrymore of B-movies, as a chain-smoking scientist who sits in his office bemusedly explaining the events of the movie to his colleagues, stiffly portrayed by veteran character actor Morris Ankrum, TV stalwart Russell Thorson, and stage and TV supporting player Robert Karnes. There is even a scene in which the men analyze the corpse of the snowman's murdered offspring, using the actual costume donated by Toho for use in the American version. And although Carradine would be captivating and entertaining reading the Yellow Pages, even he can only do so much with the material, and the result falls short of what Raymond Burr pulled off in his similarly inserted role for *Godzilla: King of the Monsters*.

Today, the Americanized John Carradine version of *Half Human* remains the only one available, and even that takes a bit of internet sleuthing. The original film that Toho made remains one of the obscure Holy Grails of *tokusatsu* cinema, with the studio keeping it under wraps due to its native depictions, which remain controversial to this day. Perhaps, eventually, it will once again see the light of day, illuminating one of Toho's critical early steps on the road to dominating monster movie cinema in the years that followed.

1957

STEVEN PEROS

"From the depths of the sea... A TIDAL WAVE OF TERROR!", promised the movie poster. At a lean 63 minutes, and given its title, I suspect audiences at the local drive-in would have been completely satisfied if *Attack of the Crab Monsters* was simply a story of a group of people stranded on an island trying to survive an onslaught of killer giant crabs. Especially because they were getting a full meal for their money, given its pairing on a double bill with the alien-in-human-skin sci-fi chiller, *Not of This Earth*. But 26-year-old writer Charles B. Griffith and 30-year-old producer/director Roger Corman, both early in their respective careers, decided that wasn't nearly enough and made the story far more sophisticated than the audience deserved. These giant crabs are also telepathic! And even that wasn't enough jeopardy because the island is also sinking! When I was a young Monster Kid watching *Attack of the Crab Monsters* on Chiller Theater in New York, I was in awe because I truly didn't know what was going to happen next in this nutty story.

After atomic testing in the Pacific, an expedition arrives on a remote island not only to study nuclear fallout effects, but also to locate an earlier expedition party that seems to have vanished without a trace following a brutal tropical storm. The new group are mostly scientists, all of whom have a special area of study, including the impossibly hairy-chested Dale Drawer (Richard Garland), token brainy female scientist, Martha Hunter (Pamela Duncan) who sports extremely sculpted eyebrows, Dr. Karl Weigand (Leslie Bradley) who inexplicably wears sunglasses both indoors and out, and quipping French scientist Jules Devereux (the always enjoyable Mel Welles). Ironically, the one man on the island team who is its most practical member, the kind of guy who loves to lug the equipment all by himself, the least professorial of all, is Hank Chapman, played by *Gilligan Island*'s very own Professor, Russell Johnson.

After setting up their respective sleeping spaces at a nearby fortified house, members of the party start to disappear, one by one. No sooner have the unsuspecting expedition members gone missing than sleeping members of the team find themselves awakened in the middle of the night, summoned by the voices of the missing scientists, beckoning them to come meet them, help them, or some other such plea. This leads the concerned expedition members to the giant crab claw clutches of the atomically irradiated crabs, which are not only twenty-five feet across, but telepathic as a result of having chomped off the heads of their victims, absorbing their memories, and transmitting their voices using nearby random metallic objects (Best not to try to figure out the science behind that process).

Once it becomes clear that there are intelligent giant crabs on the island hellbent on the demise of the expedition team, the scientists band together, trying to figure out how to defeat them. I say "them", but we never really see more than one giant crab in the frame at any given time as it is clear Corman couldn't afford a second giant crab on his purported $70,000 budget. It turns out these jumbo crustaceans are impervious to bullets and if a limb is severed, it will grow right back. To add to their problems, the giant crabs are tunneling under the island, deliberately trying to sink it so as to dispose of the pesky expedition party. These are very smart giant crabs who want to procreate and dominate, so they are not going to let these snooty scientists leave the island and tell others of their existence. Ultimately, the party is whittled down to only three surviving members: our romantic leads Garland and Duncan, and *Gilligan's Island*-bound Russell Johnson, who becomes the movie's hero, sacrificing himself by toppling an electrical tower and frying the one surviving giant crab.

Most of the beach and island scenes were shot at Malibu's Leo Carrillo State Beach and the extended cave sequences were shot at the legendary Bronson Caves, on the edge of Griffith Park, very frequently used by studios due it being easily accessible by a wide fire road, located a short walk from a residential neighborhood in Hollywood. It is best known as the famed "Bat Cave" from which the Batmobile came roaring through in TV's *Batman*, but it has been used in countless motion pictures, from low budget sci-fi/horror to John Ford's *The Searchers*.

Director Roger Corman was raised in Beverly Hills and attended Stanford University where he studied to be an engineer, like his father. He finished his degree but realized halfway through college that he didn't want to be an engineer. He started writing and selling articles and, after three years of service in the Navy, went to England to study literature at Oxford on the G.I. Bill. When he returned to Los Angeles, he wanted to write movies, but after a bad experience of being rewritten and hating the resulting movie, Corman felt that his methodical engineer brain could produce better films than he was witnessing from others. He scraped together $12,000 and produced an independent sci-fi monster movie in six days (which he did not direct) that was ultimately picked up for distribution and released in 1954 under the title, *The Monster from the Ocean Floor*, which made $110,000 in profit and solidified Roger Corman's producing career. Chief among Corman's impressive accomplishments was getting 55-year-old cinematographer, Floyd Crosby (who had shot the Gary Cooper Western classic, *High Noon*, only two years earlier!), to shoot not only this film, but many more low budget films for him over the next decade.

The next year, 1955, Corman took the director's chair himself, made five movies, and in 1956 directed eight, including *Attack of the Crab Monsters*, his third sci-fi monster movie. Released in early 1957, it was Corman's biggest hit yet, which Corman attributed to two things: the title, that was outrageous, even by his own standards, and the imaginative story, which he hashed out with Charles "Chuck"

Griffith, but which was written by Griffith. If you've never heard of Chuck Griffith, in 1998 none other than Quentin Tarantino listed him behind only *Get Shorty* novelist, Elmore Leonard, and *Chinatown* screenwriter, Robert Towne, as the three writers he admired most. Although Corman's budget and time crunch couldn't deliver the optimal realization of Griffith's work, at its core, this is a very imaginative little sci-fi monster movie, crammed with clever ideas. A few years later Griffith would write two of Corman's most sophisticated and successful movies, the horror-comedy, *A Bucket of Blood* (1959), and *The Little Shop of Horrors* (1960). Sadly, Griffith had to go to court years later to get a piece of the action from both the hit Off-Broadway musical adaptation of *Little Shop* and the subsequent hit movie made from the stage musical.

When Corman's budgets went up for his Vincent Price / Edgar Allan Poe movies, he opted for the higher profile Richard Matheson, a masterful novelist and screenwriter. Griffith would work for Corman a few more times, most notably on 1966's *The Wild Angels* (an important biker precursor to *Easy Rider*), and 1975's futuristic car racing cult classic, *Death Race 2000*. Regardless, *Attack of the Crab Monsters* holds its place as one of the earliest examples of both Griffith's and Corman's talent for clever science fiction and horror, eclipsing most of their contemporaries in terms of sly sophistication, story velocity, and sheer entertainment value.

"The Monster That Challenged The World"

1957

TRACY MERCER

The low budget, nature-runs-amok film, *The Monster That Challenged the World* is a gem of a 1950's science fiction movie that deserves a lot more love than it gets. Released in 1957, it transcends the usual formulaic sci-fi tropes of its era by crafting dimensional characters, thrilling sequences of suspense and a sustained atmosphere of legit menace.

While the premise at first blush may sound hokey to modern audiences, the execution of the idea must be seen to be believed. Mostly set at a top-secret Navy base situated next to Southern California's Salton Sea, the film opens with a giant earthquake creating a deep underwater chasm that ejects giant, prehistoric mollusks (think a slime-spewing hybrid of killer jumbo crustacean meets a punk rock caterpillar) into the sea! It turns out that the Navy base has been doing secret, atomic experiments that have exposed some of the seawater to radiation that amplifies the size and ferocity of the giant mollusks once they emerge from their prehistoric nesting spots.

"

The film kicks off when a navy skydiver, who is testing parachutes, goes missing after landing in the sea. One Navy retriever on a patrol boat dives into the ocean, never to be seen again as the second naval patrol boat officer — still on the boat — is seen screaming in terror as the shadow of an unseen monster covers his body after violently erupting from the water.

With three missing bodies to contend with, Lt. Commander John "Twill" Twillinger (played by square-jawed former Cowboy Star, Tim Holt) assembles a rescue party and finds the now abandoned initial patrol boat. Only now, it's covered in so much slime you would have thought H.R. Giger's *Alien* had been there first. The mystery takes an even more grim turn when one of the Navy officers' bodies is found, completely drained of bodily fluids, a scream frozen on his blackened visage. The corpse image remains pure nightmare fuel. With a dead body recovered and a lot of slime to bring back to the lab, Twillinger is now a man on a mission to figure out what lies beneath.

A determined commander marches into the Naval Base lab, where he hands his evidence to Dr. Jess Rogers (a terrific Hans Conried, who started off as a member of Orson Welles' Mercury Theater Company) and notices the beautiful and recently widowed Gail MacKenzie (Audrey Dalton), Rogers' secretary. There is instant chemistry between the two that plays out as a credible adult romance that, by film's end, suggests Twill, Gail, and her daughter Sandy (a precocious Mimi Gibson) might just make a 1957 modern family.

But first: Our surrogate family, with an assist from the good doctor, must work together to thwart the killer mollusks! *The Monster That Challenged the World* even has a terrific sequence that prefigures the 1980's slasher trope which dictates that when young, hot people meet up against their parents' wishes to swim (or have sex) in isolated locations, they will be killed. Here, we see a young couple pulled into the inky black depths with several shots that may remind film buffs of poor Chrissie Watkins, the first victim of the great white shark in 1975's *Jaws*.

Meanwhile, Twill takes more US Navy divers to investigate the location of the missing Navy men, where they discover a second drained body AND a giant egg of one of the mysterious creatures. The investigating divers are then attacked by another giant mollusk who kills one of them before surfacing and attempting to kill everyone on Twill's boat. Twill thinks fast and blinds the creature while also managing to retrieve the unhatched egg so Dr. Rogers can study it and determine what they are dealing with. The egg is kept from hatching in the lab's water tank through the use of temperature control.

A smart going over of current events and facts reveals that the mollusks are a massive threat to the world, as they can lay eggs quickly and can — if they get into the nearby American canal system — infiltrate the water system that irrigates the entire Imperial Valley, which then empties out into the Gulf! These giant, prehistoric mollusks, with their razor sharp teeth, have the capacity to kill on land and sea, and it quickly becomes clear that they not only challenge the world, but could potentially END it!

Plans involving setting depth charges to kill the known mollusks are put in motion. Strategies to open and then close canal locks emptying to the sea are employed to either crush or trap these monsters where they can be more easily killed. BUT, at the lab, as Gail is working the phones, trying to help connect information and people to assist in the killing of the monsters, her daughter, Sandy, enters the lab itself. The little girl, not knowing the lab has been set to be extra cold to keep the giant mollusk egg from hatching (these beasties hatch fully grown!), is concerned the test rabbits are cold, so she warms the lab temperature, thus, setting the hatching of the egg in motion. The film does a great job of creating an epic double jeopardy in the lab for the little girl and Gail sequence while the Navy men with Twill are in harm's way in the field.

The huge action set piece between Gail and her daughter fighting the giant mollusk in the Navy lab is thrilling. It also feels like it could have inspired a similar scene from James Cameron's *Aliens* where Company Man Burke traps Ripley and Newt in a med lab with the hopes of facehuggers impregnating them for the evil company's desire to birth xenomorphs for their weapons division. Back to Gail's valiant efforts: she keeps her daughter and herself alive just long enough for Twill to arrive and dispatch the mollusk with cunning. Eggs destroyed, mollusks blown up, and the surrogate family of Gail, Sandy, and Twill reunited, *The Monster That Challenged the World* ends on a positive note: The American good guys vanquish the monsters.

The love the filmmakers had for their creature feature shines through every frame. Producers Arthur Gardner and Jules Levy, along with director Arnold Laven, met as young men serving in the Army's First Motion Picture Unit during WWII. Then-Army Capt. Ronald Reagan was the personnel officer of the unit, which made training films from 1942 to 1945.

After WWII, Gardner, Levy, and Laven launched a company to critical and box office success with three films: *Without Warning, Vice Squad,* and *Down the Dark Streets*. Suddenly a hot commodity in Hollywood, the trio brainstormed ideas for *The Monster That Challenged the World* to capitalize on the sci-fi creature craze. They came up with the core idea of the movie and had scribe David Duncan outline the idea into a story document. Then, the men did something unusual for their time: They offered their brilliant secretary (and UCLA graduate) Pat Fielder, who was interested in screenwriting and had previously published children's stories, the opportunity to write the script. She delivered an elevated script that got everyone excited. The trio assembled a great cast and smartly utilized SoCal locations to produce this $250,000 film. Let's also celebrate creature designer Augie Lohman, who was coming off having just created the great white whale for director John Huston's *Moby Dick*.

While modern audiences might chuckle at the vintage trailer describing the mollusks as "The most bloodcurdling monster of the age!" one thing is for certain: this special monster film is a winner and deserves to be rediscovered.

STEVEN PEROS

The Giant Claw gets no love. If you search reviews online or find it mentioned in the pages of other learned monster movie books, you will find all sorts negativity, largely stemming from the special effects utilized to bring audiences the Kong-sized giant bird from outer space. Well, I hereby dissent with popular opinion, pronouncing it thoroughly enjoyable, and guaranteeing you this: once you see *The Giant Claw*, you will never forget it!

In the North Atlantic, electronics engineer and radar expert, Mitch MacAfee (Jeff Morrow, star of 1955's *This Island Earth* and 1956's *The Creature Walks Among Us*), is manning a test flight to study radar and its limits when he spots the fast-flying blur of a UFO "as big as a battleship". His team down below, which includes mathematician and systems analyst, Sally Caldwell (Mara Corday, star of 1955's *Tarantula!* and 1957's *The Black Scorpion*, both reviewed in *Giant Bug Cinema*), claim there is no indication on the radar of such a UFO. Better safe than sorry, an Air Force unit takes flight to investigate. When they find nothing, Mitch is read the riot act by Major Bergen (Clark Howat) who insists Mitch was playing some pathetic gag, which has resulted in one of the Air Force jets gone missing. However, when a commercial flight carrying 60 passengers also goes missing, the major changes his tune. Could there be something up there? And if so, how can it remain undetected by traditional radar, especially if it is as big as a battleship, as Mitch claims?

When Mitch and Sally take to the skies to investigate, they are buzzed by the still unseen UFO, which results in their plane crash-landing in the Canadian wilderness (Hollywood's reliable Griffith Park standing in). It's one of those convenient movie plane-crashes where both occupants survive the burning wreckage, unscathed. They are given shelter by French-Canadian farmer (Lou Merrill), who has seen the giant creature and believes it to be "La Carcagne," from Canadian folklore (a cultural factoid that just may have been made up or misquoted by the screenwriters). The couple takes a commercial flight back home, on board which we witness a seven-minute scene (mind you, that's nearly 10% of the movie's entire running time) where Mitch posits a possible pattern to these attacks while making passes at Sally, who is resistant to both his theories and advances. It's to the credit of charming chemistry between stolid Jeff Morrow and sassy Mara Corday that this scene entertains. Credit of course, should also go to writers, Samuel Newman (1959's *Invisible Invaders*) and Paul Gangelin (1943's *The Mad Ghoul*). At roughly a half-hour into the 74-minute running time, we get our first good look at the UFO, which turns out to be giant buzzard-like bird. It not only chases a plane carrying four members of a civil aeronautics investigating team, but when they bail out to escape the bird, it snaps the plane in its nostril-flaring beak, proceeding to swoop down and eat each parachuting team member in mid-air as they try to escape.

Mitch and Sally are now summoned to the office of the impossibly named General Buskirk (pronounced throughout as "Buzz-kirk", played by Robert Shayne), where Sally realizes there may be an image of the creature captured by weather balloon cameras. Sure enough, as they study the filmstrips, they see the big buzzard in all its glory, which leads them to bring out the really big guns, Lieutenant General Considine (Morris Ankrum). Any connoisseur of 1950's sci-fi knows that the situation must have gotten severe if Morris Ankrum is brought in. The authoritative, medal-laden, but always approachable Ankrum donned a military uniform or senior doctor's smock in 1956's *Earth vs the Flying Saucers*, 1957's *Beginning of the End* and *Kronos*, and 1958's *Giant from the Unknown*, reviewed in this book.

Much speculation takes place as to the origins of this big bird. As explained by one authority in the movie, the legend of La Carcagne states, "If you see the big bird, it's a sign you're gonna die. Real soon." When bullets and bombs prove useless against the flying beast, a solution is needed, so General Considine assigns Mitch and Sally to Dr. Noymann (Edgar Barrier, a veteran of Orson Welles's Mercury Theater, as well as one of the two leading men rivaling for Christine's affection in 1943's *The Phantom of the Opera*). Noymann examines one of the bird's lost feathers and finds that it "defies analysis and has no elements recognizable by man". Noymann proclaims the big bird to be from outer space and comprised of antimatter. It also has no reflective surfaces, which explains why it can't be seen on radar. In fact, it possesses an "antimatter energy screen", which is why no bullets, bombs, nor missiles can penetrate its feathery flesh. Mitch, a never-say-die electronics engineer, believes he can create a frequency that can incapacitate the antimatter energy screen just long enough for General Considine to have his Air Force boys explode the bird into one helluva down pillow. And that's exactly what they do, the executed bird plummeting into the sea, its giant claw the last thing we see before it sinks to the bottom.

The Giant Claw was a product of legendary low budget producer, Sam Katzman, who ran a bargain basement unit for Columbia Pictures, making several movies a year, back-to-back, on very low budgets and tight shooting schedules. By his own admission, he was purely a businessman and not concerned with making art. After producing the big Columbia moneymaker, *Earth vs. the Flying Saucers*, with director Fred F. Sears (who had also directed 1956's *The Werewolf* for Katzman) and special effects by the great Ray Harryhausen, Katzman wanted to do another airborne FX monster movie with Sears and Harryhausen. Columbia said yes, but when Harryhausen was either unavailable or unwilling, the legend goes that Katzman bragged about farming the special effects out to a Mexican company who came up with the much-maligned giant buzzard marionette (some suggest it looks more like a flying turkey, but why quibble-gobble?).

There does not seem to be any record of these Mexican special effects artists, and the on-screen credit lists only "Technical Effects by Ralph Hammeras and George Teague". Hammeras was 63 at the time and a veteran of Oscar-nominated special effects work as far back as 1925's *The Lost World* and as recent as Disney's epic *20,000 Leagues Under the Sea*. This was the last film for Teague, 64, whose credits go back to 1924. Whether Hammeras, Teague, an unnamed Mexican company, or the combination of all three, I side with those brave dissenters who actually find these bargain-budget effects especially fun and inventive. Sure, you can see the wires, but that ugly bird is very expressive in the closeups with flaring nostrils and glaring eyes. So, some of the planes seem like toys, but the original miniature work in the Manhattan scenes is actually very detailed (a few destruction shots were reused from *Earth vs the Flying Saucers*).

And yet, many lock-step, cynical reviewers seem to echo the prophecy of the movie itself: that the viewer does actually die just a little bit once they behold *The Giant Claw*. I wholeheartedly disagree! Once you see *The Giant Claw*'s battleship-sized turkey-buzzard from outer space (made of impenetrable antimatter, no less!), you will have lived just a little bit more than those sad moviegoers who have yet to bear witness to its glory.

1957

MIKE PEROS

I came upon *The Cyclops* recently and was drawn to it for a few reasons. One was that, as a proud English teacher of Greek descent, I was curious as to how writer/director Bert I. Gordon would incorporate the myth of Odysseus and the Cyclops into his narrative. To hear Gordon tell it, he not only knew the myth, but had taken pains to relate his screenplay to the original tale. But more about that later…

The other attractions were the cast and the setting. Not the film's setting, but the conditions under which it was made. This is a Monogram release, which was low on the Hollywood studio food chain. Yet the cast featured former MGM stars James Craig and Tom Drake, rising scream queen Gloria Talbott, and horror icon Lon Chaney Jr. Chaney rose to stardom as the dim-witted Lennie in the 1939 classic *Of Mice and Men*, and as the doomed Larry Talbot in 1941's *The Wolf Man*. Critics accused Chaney of playing variations on Lennie in low (and lower) budget films, but he delivered many solid portrayals, including his underrated turn as the Count in *Son of Dracula* (1943) and the arthritic former sheriff in *High Noon* (1952). Though his alcoholism could pose problems on the set, Chaney's performances were usually entertaining and full-bodied.

Gloria Talbott began her career as a child actress and by 1955, she was the ingénue alongside Humphrey Bogart in *We're No Angels* (an underrated gem from 1955). However, she staked a claim in our horror hearts with *The Daughter of Dr. Jekyll* (1957), *I Married a Monster from Outer Space* (1958), *The Leech Woman* (1960), and her work here. So, it may not be too hard to see what she was doing here exploring the jungles of Mexico.

As for James Craig and Tom Drake, they had similar career paths that overlapped at MGM. At RKO, Craig starred opposite Ginger Rogers in *Kitty Foyle* (1940) and *All that Money Can Buy* (1941). MGM studio head Louis B. Mayer thought Craig resembled the Air Force-bound Clark Gable, and so Craig was given leads in such films as *The Human Comedy* (1943) and *Marriage is a Private Affair* (1944, opposite Lana Turner). Unlike Craig, Tom Drake started at MGM, first in small roles, then with a lead in 1944's *Meet Me in St. Louis*, as Judy Garland's "boy next door" love interest. The end of World War II meant the return of many MGM stars and soon both Craig and Drake were relegated to leads in "B" movies and studio loan-outs. By the time of *The Cyclops*, the potential for major stardom was behind both Craig and Drake, though they were still "in the game" in either lower budget films or television.

When Chaney, Talbott, Drake, and Craig had signed for *The Cyclops* all believed it would be made for RKO which, while not a major player, still had some cachet. Soon after, it was announced that the movie would be made for Monogram, which meant a lower budget and abbreviated shooting schedule (six days). Budding auteur Bert I. Gordon, fresh off his debut feature *King Dinosaur*, declared he would do the special effects himself. These Gordon-generated effects seem to consist almost entirely of rear projections and clumsy matte shots where it is clear that none of the actors were in danger at any time.

As to the feature: *The Cyclops* has a determined Gloria Talbott searching for lost fiancée Bruce, who disappeared in the Mexican wilds three years earlier. Unlike Penelope in *The Odyssey*, she will not wait at home for her wandering fella. She is advised by a Mexican official that she can have a plane, although "No one has ever returned..." Along for the quest is James Craig's scientist, who loves Talbott, Tom Drake's hard-drinking pilot, and Lon Chaney's mining expert who hears the siren song of uranium in the terrain.

A momentarily crazed Chaney tries to take control of the plane, leading to a crash landing, and it's here in this "Mexican jungle" that the actors must share the screen with these "special effects," beginning with Craig viewing a giant lizard. After Craig and Talbott see an oversized rodent and a giant bird having a squawk, Talbott wonders why these animals are so large, while Craig opines that "it might not be safe around here." Chaney insists that Drake fly him back, but Drake, mensch that he is, says they're going to remain for Talbott's sake, since she "feels his presence."

While Chaney is the ostensible villain, it's his character who makes the most sense. When he states, "We'll be lucky if we make it out alive," that may be the booze talking, but whatever his venal reasons are, the character is right. This becomes clearer when Craig and Talbott admit to creature sightings, yet when Talbott still wants to find Bruce, Drake says he'll honor his contract with her, and even scientist Craig wants to find out why these animals are growing. Chaney utters "They're all crazy," and it's hard to disagree.

When they find a dying giant lizard, Craig cuts off some skin tissue and notes that the creature's cells grow continuously because of "something here that stimulates them." It's now two/thirds in, and still no Cyclops, though the viewer sees a towering figure looking down on the group. In short order, our heroes find the wreckage of Bruce's plane and a cave in which they find Bruce's watch. Then, the Cyclops finds *them* and as in the myth, places a huge rock across the cave entrance, blocking the exit.

The Cyclops is played by Duncan Parkin, and it was his season for playing giants, since he would be the Beast in 1958's *War of the Colossal Beast* (covered in a later chapter). His Cyclops is the real special effect here, especially the disfigured, misshapen face with its areas of sunken, seemingly melted skin. However repulsive this one-eyed giant is, what makes him a major nuisance is his constant wailing (courtesy of sound effects and the usually reliable voice-acting of Paul Frees) which makes him sound like a cyclops suffering from persistent dry heaves.

Instead of the pace picking up, there is now talk about who this Cyclops is. The un-special effects are also evident, with an outstretched hand superimposed on the foursome. After several close-ups of Chaney trying (in vain) to look in the direction of the giant hand effect, his character has a meltdown and shoots the Cyclops, who responds by swiftly killing Chaney with a giant finger.

The Cyclops then removes Talbott from the cave (with the hand taking some scenery along with her), but treats her most tenderly. This strange interlude is interrupted by a giant bird, and while the Cyclops battles this creature, Craig and Drake are able to spirit Talbott away. On their way back, Craig informs Talbott of what we already knew—that the Cyclops is indeed Bruce, and that his growth and grotesque appearance is the result of radiation seeping in to his bloodstream through a scar. (No explanation is made for the wailing.) However, the Cyclops is blocking access to the plane, so Craig shoots a flaming arrow into its eye, clearing the way for the plane to leave, and for the grieving Talbott to find solace with the comforting Craig.

One can knock *The Cyclops* for many reasons, namely the shoddy special effects and its slow pace (remarkable since the movie is a scant seventy minutes). However, it is still entertaining, as this band of seasoned performers manage to maintain the viewer's interest in the unlikely proceedings. The budget may be slim, but the four actors give it their all, with Chaney stealing most of the scenes. If only he were allowed a better exit…

1957

JUSTIN HUMPHREYS

As a kid, I was dead certain that Bigfoot had my number—that he was lurking in every wooded area near me. And growing up in Virginia, which is about 63% forests, that meant he might be practically anywhere. I doused this imaginary fire in gasoline by reading every unexplained phenomena book I could lay my hands on. Bigfoot, Mothman, the Hodak, and all those other cryptids seemed peculiarly real to me, thanks largely to all those putatively truthful books. I mean, they were by adults, so how could I doubt their veracity?

To this day, any older movie about the Sasquatch gives me a tiny, not unpleasant little jolt of recollection of my childhood terrors. The episode of "In Search Of" featuring a reenactment of a reported attack by a Sasquatch mob on some prospectors' cabin is a nostalgic rush for me. Quality has nothing to do with the effectiveness of these movies or their enjoyability. I'm a complete sucker for any drive-in movie featuring a bunch of yahoos being terrorized by some poor shmuck suffering away in a mangy ape suit, from pseudo-documentaries like *The Legend of Boggy Creek* (1972), to regional cheapies like *Creature from Black Lake* (1976). Then there's the notorious (now debunked) Patterson-Gimlin footage of "the real Bigfoot", which has its own special magic.

There are many international variations of Bigfoot, including the Chinese Wild Man and the Australian Yowie. But, most famously, going furry-hand-in-hand with Bigfoot, there's his Nepalese cousin, the Abominable Snowman or Yeti. I read all about him as a kid, as well, and of mountaineer Sir Edmund Hillary, his Sherpa guide, Tenzing Norgay, and Hillary's unsuccessful Yeti hunt. This was utterly fascinating stuff—the idea that the Sasquatch might be the hillbilly cousin of a white-haired, snow-dwelling missing link.

When I was about eight, I saw that Val Guest's *The Abominable Snowman of the Himalayas* (originally simply titled *The Abominable Snowman*) was playing on TV—on the USA Network, that trashy trailer park of 80's cable, as I recall. The title alone was a supreme lure to me. In those days, without even a VHS player, successfully catching a monster movie when it aired meant unstinting surveillance of TV listings and catch-as-catch-can luck, sometimes mid-broadcast. I lucked out on that one, and I vividly remember watching it at my grandmother's house— she had 25 or so cable channels, the height of luxury.

What I was expecting was something lurid and sensational: brave mountaineers fending off a pack of bloodthirsty Yeti that would make *The Empire Strikes Back*'s Wampa quail. Or Abominable Snowmen snarling and lunging at lone, desperate climbers, and rending them limb from limb. Scary, overt stuff— something akin to the cover art of Warren Smith's *Strange Abominable Snowmen*, only blunter and nastier. And since this was a Hammer movie, somebody like stuntman Eddie Powell would play the main Yeti, or, if it had been made a little later, Kiwi Kingston, or a little later still, Darth Vader-to-be David Prowse. I was all set to have my hackles raised at the sound of distant Yeti shrieks dimmed only slightly by the Himalayas' howling winds, followed by snarling, mayhem, and massacres.

What I *got* was a movie much too mature for me: a talky, idea-driven piece largely predicated on mood. The brilliant Nigel Kneale's script and Val Guest's subtle direction was mostly lost on me, as a kid. But I strongly recall being affected by the stark, eerie cinematography of Hammer stalwart Arthur Grant, despite his widescreen compositions being cropped in half for TV, and how good Grant made another key Hammer talent, Bernard Robinson's sets look. There are images in the film that remain seared into my memory. As skilled as Grant was at filming in color, his black and white work was superlative as well, as this movie illustrates, along with other monochrome Hammer productions like *Hell is a City* (1960).

The film follows Dr. Rollason (Peter Cushing), a botanist studying rare plants in the Himalayas, who joins up with American promoter Tom Friend (Forrest Tucker) on a search for the fabled Yeti. It quickly becomes obvious that Friend's motives are shady: he's a carny out to catch a Yeti to put it on display and exploit it (Rollason should have known better than to trust a guy named "Friend", as big a red flag as a nickname like "Honest John"). With a massive snowstorm moving in, things go from bad to worse for their expedition. Though they manage to kill a Yeti, his kinfolk turn the tables on Friend and his companions.

The moment that sticks with me the most from that childhood viewing is the sequence where a member of Friend's party, McNee (Michael Brill), stares in deadened horror as a massive, hairy Yeti hand reaches into the tent and feels around the rifles and other equipment. That moment absolutely petrified me—even more so because the rest of the monster was off-camera. I was imagining the creature based on my daydreams and nightmares. And later in the film, Friend's trapper, Shelley (Robert Brown), is confronted by Yeti in the storage cave, and the look of total terror on his face in stark black and white was exceedingly effective.

Those were the kinds of things I was seeking from the movie when I was a kid, not what Kneale and Guest delivered. As an adult, my take on the movie is, unsurprisingly, almost completely different: I enjoy the film very much, with its peculiar plot twists and unusual ideas. There are discussions of how the Abominable Snowmen are a nearly-extinct species that would inherit the earth after mankind eradicated itself in World War III or IV. And the Yeti have telepathic powers and can make people imagine they're hearing their friends' voices, a wrinkle not unlike the visions characters experience in Kneale's scripts to 1967's *Quatermass and the Pit* (covered in *Giant Bug Cinema*) and *The Stone Tape* (1972). Kneale, the mastermind of the extraordinary Quatermass movies, excelled at these kinds of concepts. And Guest directed a bona fide science fiction masterpiece, *The Day the Earth Caught Fire* (1961). These were skilled men making movies for thoughtful adults. Unlike so many films about the Sasquatch and Yeti, it's not about the creatures' bestial nature: when Rollasan encounters the creatures face-to-face, he—and we, the audience—see the *humanity* in a Yeti's face. They aren't dumb monsters, like Friend and the others thought. "What I was looking for doesn't exist," Rollasan tells his associates on returning to civilization.

So many of the reasons *The Abominable Snowman of the Himalayas* didn't work for me as a kid are also why it's a fine film for adults. It's the antithesis of all those chintzy Bigfoot and Yeti movies, except in the sense that it only reveals the monster sparingly. In the lower-end Bigfoot movies, keeping the monster largely off-camera meant the filmmakers could get by with using a third-rate gorilla suit, which wouldn't be subjected to close scrutiny onscreen. But Guest kept the creatures' presence to a bare minimum to heighten the tension.

Cushing, Tucker, and the rest of the cast are all very good, particularly Cushing, who could make lame dialogue sound good, and good dialogue sound magnificent. Although the film is a winner in many respects, its parts are better than the whole, and there are ideas in it that only partly make sense. For instance, if the Yeti are somehow more sophisticated than Man—their telepathic abilities, for instance—why have they not developed even rudimentary clothing? They have natural fur coats, yes, but the question still stands, and begs the further question:

Are Abominable Snowmen really worthy of inheriting the earth?

THE AMAZING COLOSSAL MAN

1957

STEVEN PEROS

There is a reason why this book contains five movies made by director, producer, and sometimes writer, Bert I. Gordon, who died at the age of 100 while this book was being written: Bert liked 'em BIG. In fact, his 2009 autobiography was titled *The Amazing Colossal Worlds of Mr. B.I.G.*, a copy of which he inscribed to me at Los Angeles' Monsterpalooza Convention in 2010 after I interviewed him before a packed audience: "To Steven, a good friend. Bert I. Gordon". I cherish having been asked to interview Bert by his talented daughter, Susan Gordon, who gave very natural and focused performances in her father's un-gigantic but very solid psychological thriller, *Tormented* (1960), and his perverse matricide thriller, *Picture Mommy Dead* (1966), opposite Don Ameche.

Bert Gordon's career trajectory was not unlike that of his better-known contemporary, Roger Corman (see chapter on *Attack of the Crab Monsters*). Born in Kenosha, Wisconsin, Bert was always fascinated by movies as well as the various promotional gimmicks offered to lure audiences inside. Just as he did when watching magic shows, Bert would

"

try to figure out how the tricks on stage and screen were achieved. This led him to not only be drawn to filmmaking, but also special effects wizardry. He opened a production company in St. Paul, Minnesota, exclusively making commercials, documentaries, and instructional films, but the pull of Hollywood feature filmmaking was strong, so he headed to Los Angeles. Bert knocked on lots of doors before he scraped together $18,000 and produced, shot, and edited a largely forgotten treasure-hunt picture called *Serpent Island* (1954), notable as the feature directing debut of later-Emmy-Award winning director, Tom Gries, who would go on to direct excellent movies for Charlton Heston (*Will Penny*) and Charles Bronson (*Breakheart Pass*).

After *Serpent Island*'s modest success, Bert was ready to direct, making his feature debut with *King Dinosaur* (1955). Two more hits in 1957 (*The Cyclops*, covered earlier in this book, and *Beginning of the End*, covered in *Giant Bug Cinema*) brought Bert to the attention of American International Pictures (AIP), which needed a director for a giant man movie they were developing to cash in on Universal's *The Incredible Shrinking Man* (1957). According to AIP historian, Mark McGee, in his book, *Faster and Furiouser: The Revised and fattened Fable of American International Pictures*, Roger Corman was the first on board to direct, but he and his writer, Charles Griffith (see chapter on *Attack of the Crab Monsters* for more on the Corman/Griffith collaborations), wanted to make a comedy out of the idea (perhaps akin to the tone they would later perfect in 1959's *A Bucket of Blood* and 1960's *The Little Shop of Horrors*). When Corman and Griffith exited the project, AIP brought it to Bert, who worked up a straight sci-fi tragedy, cowriting it with Griffith's occasional writing partner, Mark Hanna, with whom Griffith had just written two Corman horror films, *Not of This Earth* and *The Undead*, and would write *Attack of the 50 Foot Woman* the following year, which is also covered in this volume.

By the time Bert wrote his memoir at roughly 85 (fifty years after this movie was made), he recalled a very different genesis to the project: "I had written the idea for a film onto a paper napkin, about a man growing to the height of sixty feet, with the title   THE AMAZING COLOSSAL MAN'. The next day I met with (AIP owners) Jim and Sam in their office on Sunset, and made a four picture deal with them." Bert does not mention Hanna in his book, nor any cowriters of his films, nor was he too keen to discuss his many cowriters over the years during my interview with him, moving away from my screenwriter questions onto other topics. My sense was that Bert felt these movies were his visions, and thus he may have been frustrated that he needed more accomplished screenwriters to help him bring his visions to life or acknowledge their creative co-ownership. Whatever the case, and regardless of his varying cowriters over the years, there is no denying the consistency of Bert's vision in all of his movies, with *The Amazing Colossal Man* being a gloriously prime example.

During a plutonium bomb test, Colonel Glenn Manning (Glen Langan) becomes concerned when a truck drives into harm's way and crashes. When the bomb's detonation has a glitch, Glenn takes a heroic chance and runs to save the driver. Unfortunately, the glitch corrects itself and the bomb detonates, stripping Glenn of all his hair and covering him in third degree burns. When his skin miraculously regenerates with no scars after mere hours, Glenn is whisked to a secret military facility for study. His fiancé, Cathy (Carol Downs), does some sleuthing and sneaks in where she discovers that Glenn is now 20-feet tall! Enter Dr. Lindstrom (William Hudson, in the role usually reserved for Jeff Morrow or Richard Denning) who explains that Glenn is growing at a rate of 8-10 feet per day. By this point, parallels to *The Incredible Shrinking Man* become apparent: the agonized spouse, the atomic culprit, and the angry, self-loathing hero who was just in the wrong place at the wrong time. Just as Scott Carey in *The Incredible Shrinking Man* must live in a doll house, Glenn Manning must live in a circus tent. Screenwriter Hanna's dark sense of humor is on display when Manning mentions how he was dubbed in his high school yearbook: "The Man Most Likely to Reach the Top," well aware of the cruel irony.

Manning can't take the isolation and humiliation, so he escapes. He is also going a bit mad because his heart is growing at only half the rate of his other organs, creating blood flow problems which impede his grasp on reality as well as his sense of paranoia. This leads to the film's memorable set piece: The now-60-foot Manning's destructive parade through the Las Vegas Strip. As he heads to Boulder Dam, the scientists believe they have a serum that can stop his growth, but when they inject the jumbo needle into his shinbone, the miffed Manning removes the needle and — in a moment every Monster Kid recalls with shock —

uses it like a dart to impale the poor soldier below who had shoved it into him. Ultimately, the dementia-ridden Glenn carries Carol off to the edge of Boulder Dam where he finally realizes who she is and puts her down, now allowing the military to fire missiles at him, sending Glenn to his death (or rather, to his sequel).

The Amazing Colossal Man is a perfect example of both Bert and AIP's ingenuity in the face of tight budgets. Please see chapters on *The Cyclops*, *The Magic Sword*, and *Village of the Giants* for more on Mr. B.I.G.'s pre-1970 cinematic adventures, as well as *Giant Bug Cinema* for chapters on *Beginning of the End* (1957) and *Earth vs the Spider* (1958). Shot like a fine film noir by the great Joseph Biroc (whose exceptional films are too numerous to list), *Colossal Man* benefits from Bert's sense of pace, his effective special effects, and the sensitive performance of Glen Langan. Neither Biroc nor Langan would return for Bert's sequel, *War of the Colossal Beast*, but for more on that, dear reader, you will have to read on!

1958

LARRY BLAMIRE

When I wrote *The Lost Skeleton of Cadavra* (2001), I made sure to satirize one of my favorite monster movie elements: the setup of a forbidding or haunted place where nobody is supposed to go. Naturally, I piled on spooky place-names to the point of absurdity. But nowhere is this storytelling tool more effective than in *Giant from the Unknown*. After all, would you dare venture to… Devil's Crag?

As the film opens, citizens of the mountain town of Pine Ridge ("just a wide spot in the road") are already distressing over a series of mutilations of cattle, horses, chickens, and Old Man Banks (in that order). Plus, some sheep have vanished. Townsfolk speak of the supernatural, an ancient curse, centered in an area known as Devil's Crag. Suddenly, those lovely, tall trees and majestic mountains (Big Bear, CA, doubling for Devil's Crag) don't seem so welcoming. The locals are a distinctive lot (nobody else looked like Oliver Blake, who plays the café owner, and does anyone else think he sounds exactly like Sterling Hayden?), among them, young clean-cut Charlie Brown (Gary Crutcher), his sister Ann (Jolene Brand), and solemn Indian Joe (Billy Dix), who warns of trespassing on sacred burial ground. There's also thick-headed Sheriff Parker (Bob Steele), who persecutes rock scientist Wayne Brooks (Ed Kemmer), convinced he's responsible for all the butchery. "That man has a badge instead of a brain," explains the unflappable Wayne to new arrivals, archaeologist Professor Cleveland (Morris Ankrum) and his daughter Janet (Sally Fraser). Cleveland is looking for evidence of Vargas, aka the Diablo Giant, notorious lieutenant of actual historical conquistador, Bartolomé Ferrelo (aka Ferrer, 1499—1550). They decide to pool their resources, thus establishing a likable trio of protagonists. As we will soon find out, it's the resurrected Vargas (Buddy Baer) causing all the mayhem.

This talk of Devil's Crag, combined with chilly black and white cinematography (by the film's resourceful director, Richard E. Cunha himself) of the impressive Big Bear location, is reinforced by writers Ralph Brooke and Frank Hart Taussig, who tease the creepy tension with evocative dialogue. "Somethin' brushed against the side of my face; somethin' cold and damp," says the café owner. "It was dark as the inside of your pocket when it happened." This gives *Giant from the Unknown* the feel of a tale told round a campfire, so when our hero-trio camps at Devil's Crag, there's a nice sense of dread.

This is a monster movie at its most basic, boiled down to a headline: Monster on the Loose Kills People in Scary Remote Setting. Vargas himself is not a special effect or even a monster suit; he's just a really big guy. But he's scary and formidable. His stalking of young Ann is classic horror stuff, and the subjective camera, combined with deft editing, makes for a pretty tense scene. Even more so, his lumbering down a slope as Janet tries in vain to start the jeep still holds up as nail-biting. As Tom Weaver points out in his Film Detective Blu-ray commentary track, this is one of several times Cunha smartly punches in tight to frame-out the monster. Suddenly, you don't know where he is. Is he close? Is he right there? It's several screen seconds of nicely elevated tension. Unlike all too many low budget horrors that skimp on (what the kid in me still calls) "monster action," here we have a reasonable abundance of onscreen mayhem, particularly when Vargas hurls boulders (and not-quite-boulders) down on the hapless posse stalking him in the mountains. At one point, he picks up an attacker and hurls him, and it's pretty convincing. All of this is good stuff from a low budget filmmaker displaying sharp instincts. Even *more* impressive when you consider it was his first film.

Richard E. Cunha has become recognized as something of a cult director, due to four films which receive varying degrees of appreciation, all released in 1958: *She Demons, Missile to the Moon, Frankenstein's Daughter* and his first (and, some of us say, his best), *Giant from the Unknown*. The decision by Cunha and his producers to shoot at Big Bear (save for a few studio pickup shots) showed they were serious, and it pays off right from the very first shot: instant production value, and a look that immediately sets it apart from the majority of its 50's, low budget monster movie cousins. It's a remarkable first film, shot in six days, with much of the onscreen talent also working behind the camera. For me personally, this evokes not only seat-of-your-pants resourcefulness, but outdoor community theatre, where everybody pitches in and malingerers are not tolerated. It's scrappy, do-it-yourself stuff.

They even brought in legendary Jack Pierce (unceremoniously fired from Universal ten years earlier, where he had created all their iconic monsters) to do Baer's makeup; a subtle but effective job of making the guy look archaic and forbidding. In fact, throughout *Giant from the Unknown*, the image of Vargas is quite striking, reinforcing that black-and-white was the only choice for this film. We first see him, in one of the film's strongest moments, awakening from the ground during a lightning storm, eyes opening among the leaves. When he looms up there in the rocks, he seems chiseled from the same stone they are. The lighting makes him appear like something from a silent film, particularly *Der Golem* (1920). When we see him in striking closeup, peering through a jagged crack in the mill, he appears to be the same texture as the broken boards. And what a terrific location that mill *is*, again putting one in mind of something much older, like Dreyer's *Vampyr* (1932). Wayne's close-quarters fight with Vargas inside there is tense and nicely staged. And yes, though the giant's demise may come a bit quickly, it's a dramatic image on that bridge, and the process shot of cascading water is decent enough.

As I mentioned, Ed Kemmer, Sally Fraser, and Morris Ankrum are an engaging trio and their energy and professionalism add much to the film. Kemmer started out as Buzz Corry in the early sci-fi TV series, *Space Patrol*, and rejoined Fraser for Bert I. Gordon's *Earth vs. the Spider* (1958). Of course, Ankrum (see chapter on *The Giant Claw*) was a staple of 50's science fiction films, as both scientists and authority figures. (As a kid I always waited to see who showed up as general, Ankrum or Thomas Browne Henry, and in *Earth vs. the Flying Saucers* we got both!) Bob Steele, whose unreasonable sheriff could have taken lessons from Sheriff Jeff in *The Giant Gila Monster* (see later chapter), was a longtime movie cowboy star, but many knew him as "Duffy" on *F Troop*. Ex-heavyweight fighter, 6' 7" Buddy Baer is an impressive Vargas, and I find it interesting that the previous year, he trod similar cursed ground in one of my favorite horror-westerns, the *Cheyenne* episode, "Big Ghost Basin."

When I made *The Lost Skeleton of Cadavra*, there was one more inspiration from *Giant from the Unknown*, and that's Sally Fraser. In preproduction, I gave actress Fay Masterson a copy of the film and asked her to look at Sally's portrayal of Janet (the *daughter* of a scientist), to draw from for her portrayal of Betty (the *wife* of a scientist) in my movie. Janet's delightful innocence, her chipperness delivering such lines as "Well, it's time to load up the shovels again!" and "Next thing you'll be telling me there really *is* such a thing as suspended animation," were exactly what I had in mind, as well as her touching warmth towards her father. Fay was delighted and inspired by Sally's performance. And boy, did I get a charge when Tom Weaver passed all this along to the *real* Sally and then relayed back to me what a kick she got out of it. It was a beautiful thing. Not unlike *Giant from the Unknown*.

ATTACK OF THE 50 FT. WOMAN

1958

TRACY MERCER

The delightfully schlocky trailer for *Attack of the 50 Foot Woman* opens with the following sales pitch: "Horror! Shock! Frenzy! Devastation! As the most GROTESQUE MONSTROSITY of all... Breaks Loose!"

Really? A rich woman in a small town having marital problems with her cad husband AND who suddenly grows into a 50-foot Giant while owning her anger and power was scarier to 1950's audiences than the terrors unleashed in preceding films like: *Zombies of the Stratosphere, The Beast From 20,000 Fathoms, The War of the Worlds, Creature from The Black Lagoon, Godzilla,* the killer ants from *THEM!, Tarantula* or even the pods of *Invasion of the Body Snatchers*? If only our titular star Allison Hayes smiled more, perhaps the marketing campaign would have been kinder to her?

Ahh, but then where would the fun be in that? I would argue this film continues to live in the imaginations of film buffs in large part because of its iconic film poster. The image of a giant, sexy and scantily-clad woman straddling a freeway in a cityscape picking up a car, and sending many men running is what brilliantly sold this film in 1958 and remains an iconic image that has been spoofed and referenced in pop culture ever since. Everything from Dreamworks' 2009 *Monsters vs. Aliens* with their Ginormica character (described as a 49 Foot, 11-and-a-half-inch woman) to singer PJ Harvey's single, "50 Ft. Queenie" to The Tubes song, "Attack of the 50 Ft Woman" celebrates this film. *Sex and the City* even centered an episode where Sarah Jessica Parker's Carrie Bradshaw is fighting with her Ex, Mr. Big's new stunning wife with the title, "Attack of the 5'10" Woman". And, let's not forget that Christopher Guest directed a 1993 remake of the film starring Daryl Hannah with a decidedly feminist spin for a new generation.

But let's travel back to 1958 and talk about the original film, *Attack of the 50 Foot Woman*. At its core, this is a film about a rich heiress on the verge of a nervous breakdown who is being gaslit by a philandering husband in a small California desert town. While anchored to the 1950's patriarchal institutions and the mores of that time, this film also stands out as a rare sci-fi/horror movie of the era told from the woman's point of view.

The set-up of this 66-minute film is simple: We open on a television anchor informing us that there have been global reports of UFO sightings in the skies. Based on no logic other than the script, written by Mark Hanna (*Gunslinger* and *The Amazing Colossal Man*) saying so, the TV reporter reasons that these sightings suggest the next UFO appearance will occur somewhere in California.

Cut to Nancy Archer (Allison Hayes), who we learn is a rich lady with a knack for mental breakdowns and consuming large amounts of booze. She also has a rocky marriage to her cheating husband, Harry (a sleazy William Hudson). It seems Nancy has a $50 million estate and if her hubby can make her snap, he can have her institutionalized and take control of her vast fortune. Harry launches into his version of Operation: Gaslight the Wife!

Harry is not alone in his duplicity. He has a lover in the form of small town bad-girl, Honey (a devilish Yvette Vickers). While Harry thinks he can get his wife to crack up, it's the seductress Honey who takes a page out of *Double Indemnity*'s Phyllis Dietrichson's handbook and suggests murder of an inconvenient spouse might be the best plan.

We naturally empathize with Nancy as we see her very real run-in with a glowing orb and a giant alien who reaches for her. She escapes back to town where her out of this world tale is promptly ignored, everyone assuming she's crazy and on a bender.

Meanwhile, after two cops conclude their performative search, they send a frustrated Nancy home. Nancy implores Harry to believe her tale. She begs Harry to go with her and look for evidence of her sighting. She promises to voluntarily check herself into a sanatorium if they find nothing. Harry agrees and they drive back to the desert location. When the giant male alien DOES appear, Harry is gobsmacked and fires his gun at the hulking figure. No harm befalls the alien and Harry leans into his cowardice by driving off, leaving Nancy to meet her fate with the giant alien.

Assuming there was an "Alien Ex Machina" solution provided to the dispatching of his inconvenient wife, Harry's hopes for a rich life with Honey are quickly dashed when Nancy is found in a strange state sometime later. The same Dr. Cushing (Roy Gordon) who told Nancy to get back with her cheating husband for her own mental well-being, now feels he should sedate Nancy and do a series of tests before she is carted off to a life of presumed confinement.

With Nancy's $50 million still in play, Honey has convinced Harry it is easiest to simply murder Nancy in her sleep with a fatal injection so they can get on with their plans to be together and be filthy rich. BUT, that noir-sy plot gets shelved when Harry enters his bedroom only to find that Nancy has now, we assume because of the touch of the giant alien, transformed into a sleeping giant version of herself!

But like all sleeping giants, Nancy awakens! We have to assume she's somehow fashioned a bikini-like outfit out of her bed linens that must have the same elasticity as Bruce "Hulk" Banner's purple pants. What's curious is that we don't actually see Nancy as our 50 Foot Woman unleashed from her restraints until 56 minutes into this 66-minute film. Up until that point, the film is mostly a gaslighting exercise juxtaposed against scenes from a sad marriage, with everyone but Nancy's loyal butler working against her. Her doctors, local law enforcement, her husband, and all the men who cover for Harry's philandering ways, are now directly in her line of fire.

The trailer warned us, *"Attack of the 50 Foot Woman*: incredibly huge with incredible desires for love and vengeance! Death and Desire!

A rampage of Destruction! Science-Fiction Reaches a NEW HIGH in TERROR!" And that pretty much sums up our ending. The small town sees Nancy leaving disaster in her wake as she works her way to the local bar and grill where she murders Honey by crushing her under debris. The film rapidly comes to a conclusion when Nancy, still in love with Harry, picks him up and starts to walk away from the authorities who are now firing their guns at her to no effect. However, when the sheriff fires a shotgun that blows up a nearby transformer, it kills Nancy and her no good, double-crossing Harry.

While the model work and VFX are silly (papier mâché hands were never scary), the performances mostly wooden, and the character work about as deep as Formica—there is something undeniably fun about this film. Elsa Lanchester appeared as the titular star of 1935's *The Bride of Frankenstein* for only about 7 minutes (10 if you count her double role as Mary Shelley) but in those fleeting screen moments, The Bride emerged a true icon of horror. I would suggest in large part because of the poster art and the final minutes of this film, Allison Hayes' 50 Foot Woman achieves similar iconic screen immortality in the science fiction genre. All Hayes' Nancy asked for was to be believed and loved as a woman. How tragic that those desires somehow made her the monster -- "the most GROTESQUE MONSTROSITY" -- in this fantastical 1958 tale.

WAR OF THE COLOSSAL BEAST

1958

STEVEN PEROS

Released on June 15th, 1958, eight months after *The Amazing Colossal Man*, maverick low budget filmmaker Bert I. Gordon actually made two more movies between *Colossal Man* and its sequel, *War of the Colossal Beast*. Those movies were *Earth vs the Spider* (reviewed in *Giant Bug Cinema*) and *Attack of the Puppet People*, which was released on a double bill with this movie. Collectively, that makes four movies Bert made for American International Pictures (AIP) in less than one year. It was quite a busy and successful time for Mr. B.I.G., a nickname later given to him by Forrest J. Ackerman, Editor of *Famous Monsters of Filmland Magazine*, which Bert liked so much that he used it as part of the title of his memoir in 2009.

Despite being shot so soon after the first film, there is very little holdover of cast or crew in this sequel. George Worthing Yates is credited with the screenplay, from a story by Bert, the identical credit the two men share on *Attack of the Puppet People*. Previously, Yates had shared writing credit on two of special effects master Ray Harryhausen's most notable 1950's films, 1955's *It Came from Beneath the Sea* (reviewed in this volume) and *Earth vs the Flying Saucers* (1956), as well as story credit on the 1954 giant ant classic, *THEM!* (covered in *Giant Bug Cinema*). The cinematographer this time around is Jack Marta, a veteran of nearly 200 movies before shooting Bert's *Beginning of the End* (1957) and *Earth vs the Spider* (1958), making this their third film together. Marta would move on to bigger studio movies in the final phase of his career, shooting the Oscar-winning *Cat Ballou* (1965) as well as the Neil Simon comedy, *Plaza Suite* (1971).

Oddly, none of the same cast and only one of the characters return in this sequel. As you may recall from the earlier chapter, in the final moments of *Colossal Man*, Colonel Glenn Manning was shot by the military and fell to his presumed death from Nevada's Boulder Dam. But as this movie begins, Miguel (Robert Hernandez), a terrified teenage pickup truck driver in Guavos, Mexico is fleeing from someone or some… *thing*. Miguel winds up in a hospital bed in shock and his pickup truck is missing as though plucked into the air, given the lack of tire tracks.

Back in the US, the story is heard on the news by Joyce Manning (Sally Fraser), Colonel Manning's sister, who has always held out hope that Glenn somehow survived the fall, especially since his body was never found. Could he have floated downriver to Mexico and be responsible for carrying the teen's pickup truck away? She contacts her unbelieving military liaison, Major Mark Baird (Roger Pace), and he reluctantly accompanies Sally to Guavos to visit Miguel, who is still in a state of shock in the hospital, but who awakens long enough to yell "Ogre!" in Spanish. Could the ogre be her beloved brother?

Joyce and Mark venture to where the teen's pickup truck was last seen and head into the nearby mountains where they find a food delivery truck graveyard. Moments later, the culprit rears his horribly scarred and battered head — Colonel Manning, played this time by Duncan "Dean" Parkin (who had a similarly grunting, bald-domed, one-eyed giant role in Bert's *The Cyclops*, reviewed in an earlier chapter). The fall from Boulder Dam has left part of his skull exposed, including a hollowed eye socket. It's an effectively gruesome makeup, created by Jack H. Young (who went on to be part of the makeup team on both

David Cronenberg's *The Brood* and Francis Ford Coppola's *Apocalypse Now*), that also disguises the fact that this is a different actor, allowing for flashbacks to the earlier film, with scenes showing actor, Glen Langan as Colonel Manning. "He's a colossal freak. And he's my brother," Joyce says with curious pride.

One story element never discussed in the sequel, but worth noting, is the status of Glenn's previously stated dire medical condition. In the prior movie, we are told that unless Glenn's growth is stopped, he will die within days because his heart is growing at half the rate of his other organs. An enormous needle with a test serum is injected into his bone in the last reel of the original, but we never learn whether it worked, largely because we are more focused on the gruesomely effective impaling death of the poor soul who did the injecting. But now, with 60-foot Glenn grunting, destroying, and foraging like a pro, we realize that clearly, the serum worked. Ah, the thankless role of scientific advancement in 1950's sci-fi films!

Since Glenn will eat anything put in front of him, it is decided to bake heavy doses of chloral hydrate into loafs of bread, load them into a van, and have Glenn devour the bread in order to knock him out. This will allow them to capture him, bring him to Los Angeles, and try to help him. Clearly, they learned a lesson or two from the six-foot hypodermic needle mishap in the earlier film. After all, even if he got angry again, it would be tough for him to impale anyone with a loaf of bread. The plan works without a hitch, and soon after, Glenn finds himself strapped down inside a Los Angeles-area airport hangar where Mark, Sally, and Dr. Carmichael (Russ Bender) try to cure his amnesia by showing him filmed images of his past (essentially, footage from *Colossal Man*). Plagued by nightmares, Glenn breaks out of his shackles and escapes, killing Carmichael, and making his way to Griffith Park which, miraculously, is doubling for… Griffith Park! I say miraculously because as any connoisseur of 1950's sci-fi knows, Griffith Park was used to double for Canada, Mexico, alien planets, and everywhere in between. It's almost shocking to see the park play itself, as it so memorably did four years earlier in *Rebel Without a Cause* (1954).

Glenn rears his head at Griffith Park's famed Observatory, which is particularly packed this night, including a busload of school kids who are taking an inordinate amount of time to board and get the heck out of there. Cue Glenn, who seizes the bus and lifts it into the air. Sally breaks through the police barricade and begs him to put it down. Finally recognizing his sister and calling her by her name (his one line of dialogue), Glenn complies and then sadly eyes a nearby electrical power line, which he deliberately grasps in both his hands, committing suicide via electrocution. At this moment, the black & white film turns to full color as Glenn fries. This was a short-lived gimmick for AIP at this time, which they utilized effectively here and in the climaxes of two other 1958 horror movies, *How to Make a Monster* and *The Return of Dracula*.

An entertaining entry, *War of the Colossal Beast* is not the *Godfather II* of The Colossal Man Saga. While it is fun to watch the two movies back-to-back (as I just did), *Colossal Beast* is the lesser of the two films, but at just 69 minutes, it certainly flies by. With Glenn a grunting mute for most of the running time, it doesn't have the angst or tragedy of its predecessor, but it does have a colorful and literally shocking finale in Griffith Park, so let's be thankful for small miracles of the colossal variety.

THE 7th VOYAGE OF SINBAD

1958

TRACY MERCER

> *From the land beyond beyond,*
> *From the world past hope and fear,*
> *I bid you, Genie, now appear!*

Any film lover would be hard-pressed to name a movie that better showcases what is cinematically possible in terms of capturing the adventure and romance of fantasy storytelling than *The 7th Voyage of Sinbad*. This film is like childhood wonder personified, wrapped up in a gorgeously over-the-top Technicolor bow that can make even the most cynical of adults flashback to a time of youthful joy. It is also worth noting that in 2008, this classic was selected for preservation in the United States National Film Registry by the Library of Congress because it was deemed to be "Culturally, historically, or aesthetically significant."

While well-directed by Nathan Juran, this opus is best remembered as a Ray Harryhausen film. Harryhausen being the ground-breaking visual effects wizard who was the conjurer of awe-inspiring creatures and designer of mythic worlds (see earlier chapters on *Mighty Joe Young* and *It Came from Beneath the Sea*).

The 7th Voyage of Sinbad was Harryhausen's first color film and the first entry in his Sinbad trilogy, which also included *The Golden Voyage of Sinbad* (1973) and *Sinbad and the Eye of the Tiger* (1977).

It also marked his first foray into "Dynamation," defined as the full color widescreen stop-motion animation technique that became Harryhausen's signature.

7th Voyage was a Columbia Pictures release starring the beautiful, if not slightly wooden, Kerwin Mathews and Kathryn Grant, who were both under studio contract. Both performers were as American and modern as can be, yet were dropped into this tale of whimsy and swashbuckling fun set in ancient, far off lands. The plot consists of a series of scenes roughly connected to get audiences to the next breathtaking Dynamation set piece. And as gorgeous as this film looks, we also need to talk about the incredible score by New York-born maestro Bernard Herrmann, who started his film scoring career with Orson Welles' directorial debut, *Citizen Kane*. Best known for his filmic collaborations with Alfred Hitchcock on classics like *The Man Who Knew Too Much, North by Northwest, Psycho, The Birds*, and *Marnie*, Herrmann also worked with directors as far ranging as Francois Truffaut, Brian DePalma, and Martin Scorsese. It's notable that Hermann also collaborated with Harryhausen on *Mysterious Island, The 3 Worlds of Gulliver*, and *Jason and the Argonauts*.

Now, let's get into the plot of this unfaithful take on Arabian Nights romanticism mixed with more than a dash of Greek mythology and a shot of high seas adventure! We enter a world rife with territorial tensions and with sailor Sinbad trying to get back home to Baghdad with Parisa, Princess of Chandra, who is the daughter of a neighboring Sultan. Sinbad hopes that by marrying her — and he does truly, madly, deeply love her — he can also help create peace between two warring territories. His best-laid plan is delayed when his ship lands on the island of Colossa for food and supplies to finish their journey. While infamous for being the home of murderous Cyclops, Colossa is also where Sinbad meets the shady magician, Sokurah (played by a wonderfully arch Torin Thatcher). A magical lamp is the secret to many of Sokurah's powers and he loses it in a battle that sees him fleeing Cyclops only to be saved by Sinbad who puts him on his ship and brings him to Baghdad.

Obsessed with getting his lamp back, because it contains a Genie who can grant wishes, Sokurah pleads with the Caliph of Baghdad to send him back to Colossa. He even tries to use a party trick of turning

Princess Parisa's handmaiden into a snake-like being — which feels like a visual warm up for Harryhausen's 1981 *Clash of the Titan*'s Medusa — but Sokurah's wishes and pleas to be returned home are ignored. The clearly duplicitous sorcerer then puts a spell on the Princess which shrinks her to Lilliputian scale. This development obviously threatens Sinbad's marriage and peace between the two kingdoms. Sokurah, who is clearly behind the spell (though somehow, no one quite seems to grasp this obvious fact), convinces Sinbad to take him back to Colossa because only a piece of an eggshell of a Roc found on Colossa can be used to counteract the spell on the now miniature Princess.

Driven by his passion to save his lady love and restore peace, Sinbad agrees to trek back to Colossa with the wicked magician in tow. And what a voyage it turns out to be! The film clips along at a dynamic pace packed with sequences of fantastical creatures and life-threatening obstacles for Sinbad and his crew to overcome. After vanquishing some would-be mutineers, Sinbad and his crew arrive back on Colossa to begin the search for the Cyclops with the magic lamp in earnest. Setbacks to the quest occur when Sinbad and some of his men get captured by a Cyclops and dropped into a giant cage. Luckily, our plucky miniature Princess manages to both free the men and enter the magic lamp, where she befriends the boyish genie, Barani (played by 12-year-old, Richard Eyer). He teaches her how to summon him with the promise that if he helps the princess and our hero escape, they will liberate him from the lamp that is his prison.

After the princess helps Sinbad escape, he defeats a Cyclops by blinding him and luring him over a cliff to his death, but not before he also retrieves the magic lamp. No fool, Sinbad tells Sokurah that unless he reverses the spell on the Princess, he will not have the lamp. Next, Sokurah leads our heroes to a nesting place of a two-headed Roc. The hungry men wind up cracking a Roc egg and killing the chick inside for food. Ultimately, Sinbad, with the knowledge the Princess got from Barani, summons the genie and uses his help to transport to Sokurah's fortress where he has taken the princess. It is here that a legendarily grand set piece featuring my favorite Harryhausen creation is first seen: a marvelous, swashbuckling skeleton (under Sokurah's command). This creature would give the silver screen's first action hero, Douglas Fairbanks Sr. a run for his money! With much effort, Sinbad bests the skeleton, gets Sokurah to return the Princess to her normal size, and leads our heroes nearly back to their ship when they encounter another Cyclops. Sinbad releases a fire-breathing dragon which fights and kills the Cyclops before sending the beast to dispatch the villainous Sokurah. Our heroes make good on releasing the helpful genie Barani by throwing the lamp into flowing lava. In return, Barani decides to stick with Sinbad as a crew member. As a coda, we also learn Barani has gifted Sinbad and Parisa the Cyclops' treasure trove as a wedding present. We fade out with our heroes sailing into the future, ready for their next adventure.

Harryhausen's epic tales have served as childhood inspiration to generations of budding filmmakers. Most notably, the love of the hero's journey and the big swing for epic adventures and romance dot the landscapes of the best films created by George Lucas and Steven Spielberg. However, even those two trailblazing filmmakers cannot lay claim to being "hands on" in generating mind-blowing effects. Obsessed with the smallest of details in his stop-motion Dynamation work, it was typical for a sequence lasting a few minutes on screen to take Harryhausen months to perfect. That's because he worked on his creatures alone, imbuing them with celluloid life one frame at a time. His legendary process of creation even caused his producer Charles H. Schneer to insure Harryhausen's hands for one million dollars. Even now, when one escapes into *The 7th Voyage of Sinbad*, you can see Schneer's investment was worth every penny.

THE KiLLER SHREWS

1959

LARRY BLAMIRE

I think that in defending what is widely considered a "bad movie", we are really defending ourselves. It's almost like we don't want to look like… oh… an idiot. But that's only part of it. Mostly, I think we take on the role of self-righteous movie avenger because we genuinely love these poor little misunderstood cinematic children. So, of course, we want the world to love them, too.

The Killer Shrews is like some weird sweater I liked as a kid. As an adult, I suddenly saw it for the ridiculous thing that it was and could have a good laugh about it. Yet, somehow, some way, I was still able to fit into the damned thing. I could squeeze into that Monster Kid mindset and enjoy it for what it was, in the spirit with which it was made.

Captain Thorne Sherman (James Best) and first mate Rook (Judge Henry Dupree) are stranded on a small island by a hurricane after delivering supplies to its only inhabitants: a handful of people at a research station, including Marlowe Craigis (Baruch Lumet), his daughter Ann (Ingrid Goude), assistant Radford Baines (Gordon

"

McLendon), resident jerk Jerry Farrell (Ken Curtis, pre-Festus on *Gunsmoke*) and servant Mario (Alfred DeSoto). Their experimentation has resulted in (as is often the case) large, ravenous shrews that threaten to overrun the island. Cue the fun.

The Killer Shrews, and its double bill companion piece, *The Giant Gila Monster* (see following chapter), were produced in Texas at the same time by radio broadcaster McLendon and actor and former Sons of the Pioneers singer Curtis, with greatly-respected special effects man, Ray Kellogg at the helm. In the case of the former film, that very cheapness may have informed its ability to create suspense; the basic dread stemming from characters trapped in isolation. It might also be the first sci-fi/horror film where the principals are holed up inside some sort of compound (later a standard trope, particularly in the glut of zombie movies and television), unless we consider the houses in the earlier Roger Corman films *The Day the World Ended* (1955) and *Attack of the Crab Monsters* (1957). In *The Killer Shrews*, the high fence suggests a mini-Fort Apache, reinforcing the idea that this is about people under siege. To a kid, it might be the most involving kind of monster movie. It projects a "we're in here, they're out there" mentality that is both scary and comforting, enhanced by an almost constant howl of winds outside. We're only safe if we stay put within claustrophobic, mottled walls that remind one of Carl Dreyer's *Vampyr* (1932) or the early experimental films of horror movie director, Curtis Harrington.

And the outside, by the way, is one bleak place. This is one of those dismal-looking black-and-white films that makes every day look overcast, even when we see shadows and sunlight. The trees are bare, the woods sparse, like nothing could live or grow there. An island of dread. Given such trappings, it almost doesn't matter what's out there. The "other" can be less than convincing and still create dread. And here, *less than convincing* is the hurdle.

Much has been made of the masked doggies who fill the title roles; a case of miscasting that even the finest canine acting cannot overcome and arguably, the film's greatest detriment. However, I believe there are a number of things that help counter this issue. For one, the rapidity of the action adds a certain frantic quality to the film. But more than that, and what I think ultimately sells the dog-shrews, is when they're seen in conjunction with a hand puppet (and, no, I never thought I'd say those words). It may be aided by its own crudity, but this is one nasty-looking piece of work. With mangy fur, glistening dead black eyes and monster teeth, they support the script's mutation angle, reminiscent of those mystery things that have washed up in recent years on Montauk and elsewhere. The most effective shots in the film are those frenetic closeups of (let's call him) the shrew-puppet-thing desperately trying to push through cracks in the wood, a toothy snout here, an eye in a knothole there. And then, there's our clearest view, when Thorne shoots the one that fatally (and in a surprisingly graphic way) bites Mario, and the thing's head slowly drops. Lay down some sweet chittering/squealing on the soundtrack (recorded no doubt by deranged monkeys), and these babies have quite the freakish energy.

A couple of scenes put me on edge as a kid. While Thorne enjoys the relative safety of the compound, Rook is left tending the boat. As the island's dangers become more and more obvious, our concern for him rises, so when he comes ashore, we're already filled with apprehension. After unloading a revolver into the shrews, he climbs a tree to escape them, a tree we know is way too small. But his cries for help are whipped away by the storm, and the tree slowly goes down, dumping poor Rook out of sight in the brush where we hear his screams.

The other scene really stuck in my craw as a kid is when Thorne and Jerry go to check on Rook and the boat, and the latter chooses this inopportune moment to turn a rifle on the hero. Jerry then panics and runs back to the stockade, locking the gate, leaving Thorne to pound on it as shrews bear down. Knowing at this point that their very bite is venomous makes it all the more suspenseful, let alone reprehensible.

The film has a climax of great invention, courtesy of writer Jay Simms, that I would call unique among contemporary horror movies. This is of course, the makeshift "tank" of four 50-gallon drums lashed together to provide passage from the compound to the relative safety of the water. By placing the protagonists right in the midst of the monsters and making our heroes awkwardly duck-walk for their lives, it effectively generates some serious anxiety for both the characters and the viewer.

I've always liked James Best, an actor of great flexibility. Just prior to this film he was memorable as a cold-blooded killer in Budd Boetticher's *Ride Lonesome* (1959) and before that, the hapless Tom Folliard in Arthur Penn's *The Left Handed Gun* (1958). Genre fans know him from two fine *Twilight Zone* episodes, "Jess-Belle" and "The Last Rites of Jeff Myrtlebank," (a wonderful showcase for him), as well as the brilliant *The Alfred Hitchcock Hour* adaptation of Ray Bradury's "The Jar," directed by the great Norman Lloyd. His credibility as Thorne Sherman does a lot of the heavy lifting, and let's face it, those endless drinking and talking scenes can use it. Judge Henry Dupree is engaging in his brief role as Rook. Ingrid Goude is lovely as Ann and gives a passable performance, while Baruch Lumet (father of director Sidney Lumet) is a convincingly earnest scientist.

The producers themselves fare quite well. As Baines, Gordon McLendon maintains a likably awkward eccentricity and has the film's most touching moment. As Thorne's bitter rival for Ann, Ken Curtis goes in the opposite direction, about as far as he can be from his iconic portrayal of Festus on the long-running *Gunsmoke*. Jerry is the type of crumb who seems there to point up all the hero's good traits (cowardly where Thorne is brave, selfish where Thorne is selfless, etc.). The final shots of Jerry standing alone on a rooftop with a shotgun, looking almost defiant as the drum-tank waddles off, are quite strong. Until he realizes he's about to be left all alone on the island.

Then he runs and gets eaten.

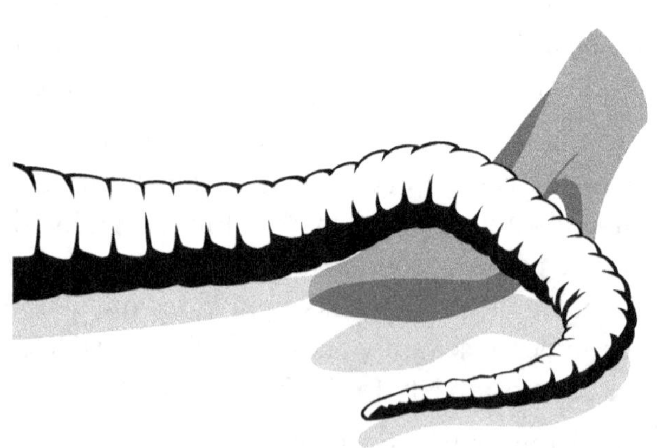

THE GIANT GILA MONSTER

1959

LARRY BLAMIRE

When it comes to monsters, teenagers never catch a break. Nobody believes them. Sometimes they even get the blame. *Invasion of the Saucer Men* (1957), *The Blob* (1958) and *Earth vs. the Spider* (1958): What do all these movies need? Fair-minded law enforcement, that's what. They need… Sheriff Jeff, played by Fred Graham, the stand-up guy who represents the law in *The Giant Gila Monster*.

A teen couple disappears from a small rural community, and our only clue is an enormous lizard foot seen descending towards camera. Local Sheriff Jeff (Graham) and teen hot-rodder and all-around decent guy Chase Winstead (Don Sullivan) lead the search, eventually discovering that a giant Gila monster is responsible and must be stopped.

As one might surmise from its creative team—producers Gordon McLendon and Ken Curtis, director Ray Kellogg, writer Jay Simms (from a Kellogg story)—*The Giant Gila Monster* is the companion to *The Killer Shrews* (see previous chapter), both shot in Texas at the same time, playing the drive-in circuit together.

It may sound odd, but in a way, this is a movie about friendship. Much screen time is devoted to Sheriff Jeff and tow-truck driving

Chase putting together clues as they investigate a series of increasingly suspicious incidents; kind of an amiable, relaxed, low-budget police procedural, peppered with convincing small talk about cars and engines and locals. There's even some delicate discussion (maturely handled) about teen pregnancy, concerning the two kids they believe may have run off. This easy banter is underplayed by Sullivan and veteran actor-stuntman Graham (the cop who falls off the roof at the beginning of Hitchcock's *Vertigo* the previous year) and has a nice father-son quality. Most importantly, these two characters form something of a linchpin between the town's teens and adult authority. They are the common ground, and their mutual respect keeps the lid on. Chase's sincere, well-meaning influence keeps the young hot-rodders in line, while the sheriff placates (and sometimes calls out) the more narrow-minded adults (mostly, the missing boy's father, the obstreperous Wheeler, played by Bob Thompson). "It's never any trouble looking after kids," the sheriff tells the concerned (but more understanding) parents of the missing girl. But it's the sheriff's faith in Chase that buys the kids that benefit of the doubt.

As you might imagine, this gives *The Giant Gila Monster* a solid community framework into which to drop its monster. Townsfolk interactions are richly detailed. Chase and his boss, Compton (Cecil Hunt), talk cars and towing. The sheriff lets Chase retrieve parts off a totaled wreck to use on his hot rod. Chase strives to protect girlfriend Lisa (French Miss Universe contestant Lisa Simone) from being deported by Wheeler, and Lisa, in turn, pays for his little sister's (Janice Stone) leg braces. Veteran character actor Shug Fisher brings his unique flavor to local rascal Harris who refuses to sell his jalopy to Chase for hot rod conversion. When Fisher chirps "You're talkin' like my foot's asleep" my mind jumps to the film's producer, Ken Curtis, who frequently used that same phrase as Festus on the long-running *Gunsmoke*. Curtis and Fisher were buddies going way back to their Sons of the Pioneers days (the latter does get to sing an amusing little ditty at the wheel of his jalopy). Fisher himself uttered the phrase yet again years later in a late 60's *Cimarron Strip* episode.

The accumulation of strange events and the ensuing investigation are enriched by Jay Simms' entertaining dialogue. "I ask you what time it is, and you tell me how to build a clock," says Sheriff Jeff, interrogating an intoxicated Harris. "I demand a *soberty* test," remarks the latter. "Let me have that patrol car," offers Chase. "I'll turn it into a slingshot that can catch anything." The search for the missing teens and the giant Gila also benefits from the same sparse, scrubby-looking locations as *The Killer Shrews*, used to particular advantage in the ominous opening narration as Wilfred M. Cline's camera pans a forbidding, blasted landscape. When Chase, Lisa, and another couple split up to investigate a ravine for the missing teens, this terrain gives the scene far more suspense than it may deserve. Eventually, the clues add up to the impossible. "What batters a car around like it was a toy?" wonders Sheriff Jeff. Interestingly enough, in lieu of a scientist, it's left to him to dig into the science of the thing, arriving at the possibility that a combination of glands, change in diet and "certain salts washed into the soil" could be responsible for the Gila monster's mutated size.

The Giant Gila Monster has the distinction, for me, of being the very first favorite monster movie of my Monster Kid son, Griffin, several years ago when he was 8 or so. No wonder, really. It's simple, direct, and just so darned engaging! Of course, his focus was (as any kid's would be) on the title character, who was evidently not a Gila monster at all but its larger cousin, the Mexican beaded lizard. Of course, the question on everyone's lips is… "How's his acting?" When Chase and Sheriff Jeff are examining clues regarding a missing hitchhiker, we see the creature watching from the bushes. Let it be said here and now that this may well be *the quietest and most patient giant monster in screen history.*

I find the lizard scenes, in their own modest way, acceptable enough to enjoy the central conceit. The scale of vegetation, dirt and road is reasonably appropriate, and the quality of the miniatures elevates that even more. The train wreck may not give the earlier *The Black Scorpion*'s similar scene (spectacular by comparison) a run for its money, but I still find it surprisingly good. And if the bridge and railroad cars are fine, the automobiles are even better. The car models used for the barn dance scene are quite handsome and nicely detailed, helping set up *The Giant Gila Monster*'s most iconic 1950's moment, when teens, Rock & Roll, and monster collide (not unlike the gymnasium scene in *Earth vs. the Spider*). It's the "money shot" where the giant lizard busts its head through the wall (some decent miniature boards) as teenagers go from dancing to their hearts' content to screaming for their lives. My only wish is that the tune playing was not a reprise of Chase's "Mushroom Song," but his more rockin' studio number that we hear a bit of when DJ Steamroller Smith (Ken Knox) spins a platter. In that song (possibly titled "Gold and Fire"), Don belts out "baby, I'm made'a that'a way," punched up by a nice layer of reverb.

Don Sullivan jumped from his hot rod for real when they shot the film's climax, as Chase sends the monster a "nitro express," and both beloved car, and lizard (or models of them), go up in fine style. And perhaps the human capper to all this is that the obstinate Mr. Wheeler sees the light, not only giving props to Sheriff Jeff, but offering Chase a job, seeing that the latter's boss, garage owner Compton, became lizard food.

As for Don Sullivan himself (who passed away in 2018), this film, *The Monster of Piedras Blancas*, and *Teenage Zombies* (all 1959) have cemented him something of a cult following, and deservedly so. An ex-marine and Korean War veteran, he was not exactly a kid when he made *The Giant Gila Monster*, yet he fits in just fine. His Chase Winstead carries a whole lot of this picture, and, if his interviews are any indication, it's *his* natural amiability that shines through. He, like Chase, seems to have been a decent humble guy. And that's a nice way to be remembered.

THE 30 FOOT BRIDE of CANDY ROCK

1959

MIKE PEROS

When I was a wee lad, I had a number of boyhood crushes, among them Diana Rigg (Mrs. Peel!), Julie Newmar (Catwoman) and Barbara Eden (Jeannie). I've also been a fan of madcap physical comedy and remember seeing, within the span of a week, *It's a Mad, Mad, Mad, Mad World* (1963), *Who's Minding the Mint?* (1967), and *The Great Race* (1965). Two of them may have been overlong but I've always found these films to be delightful with many magic moments. The one actress common to all three is the lovely Dorothy Provine. She's the moral center of both *Mad, Mad World* and *Who's Minding the Mint?*. In *The Great Race*, Provine has a guest appearance and performs a bawdy, show-stopping number which momentarily steals Natalie Wood's thunder as Tony Curtis' hero seems as attentive as the audience. I really liked this actress, who could project sincerity, albeit with a slight edge, and who could hold her own with the best comic actors (as with Jack Lemmon in 1963's *Good Neighbor Sam*).

So, when I first saw *The 30 Foot Bride of Candy Rock* on TV halfway through one afternoon after school, it was because I spotted a giant Dorothy Provine showing tenderness toward her new, normal-sized hubby, the great screen comedian, Lou Costello. And I watched it till the end, catching up with the exposition about a year later. (This was before VCRs, DVRs and streaming, when every anticipated movie was akin to an event that if missed, might not be repeated for a long, long time).

This 1959 film marked Lou Costello's first (and only) film appearance after his break-up with long-time partner Bud Abbott. Costello had appeared on *The Steve Allen Show* and put in an affecting portrayal on television's *Wagon Train* but this Columbia release, directed by Sidney Miller, was his first time carrying a movie on his own. He plays rubbish collector/inventor Artie Poinsetter who lives with his dog Corporal and an extremely resourceful computer named Max (which has Costello's voice). Costello's Artie spends much of the early footage getting rebuffed by the pompous, patronizing "Uncle Raven," played by sitcom veteran Gale Gordon, who plans to be the Governor (one feels for that state) and is the subject of a TV profile. Costello's Artie shows up during filming, which sends Gordon's Raven alternately into fits of fury and forced contrition (when he's being observed by the reporter). These comic bits, amusing at first, overstay their welcome, since Gordon's slow-burn tends to be repetitive.

What really burns Raven is that the unassuming Artie has managed to sneak Uncle Raven's live-in niece Emmy Lou (Ms. Provine) out on a number of dates, confounding Raven and impressing the impressionable Emmy Lou. Before you can say "Holy May-December! Costello's gotta be at least twenty years older than Dorothy!" Indeed, he was… twenty-nine years older, to be precise. Costello was born in 1906 and was around fifty-two when the film was being shot in December, 1958, while Ms. Provine, born in 1935, would have been twenty-three. However, Lou Costello's on-screen characters always displayed a youthful (some might say childlike) vitality. Though Costello appears older than in his prime, opposite Abbott, that energy is largely present and he seems younger than his years. More importantly, it is Provine's Emmy Lou who is doing all the pursuing, pushing a reluctant Artie to get married. It's a strategy that worked for Audrey Hepburn and Gary Cooper in the previous year in the 1957 *Love in the Afternoon*, and it works here.

The reason that Artie is so reluctant to marry has to do with his perceived lack of stature and success. Artie considers himself a nobody, and though he can spin scientific terms and formulas with ease in front of Emmy Lou, he can't seem to spit out a coherent sentence in front of his nemesis Uncle Raven or any of the town's established citizens. Emmy Lou persists while Artie protests. When Max proclaims "No marriage ever! Work now!" (Max the computer, with Costello's voice, is almost like Artie's raging id, and the film doesn't pursue the comic possibilities of Max doing/saying what Artie is incapable of.), Emmy heads for the nearby hills (once again, as per earlier chapters, there's radiation in them thar hills), and she suddenly sprouts to thirty feet.

Emmy's sudden growth results in a few funny scenes, as well as a touching moment. When Artie pleads with Raven because Emmy Lou has grown "so big," Raven concludes she is pregnant and to keep Artie quiet, he arranges for Magruder the minister to immediately marry the pair. And so, in a bridal outfit consisting of a silken parachute, Artie and Emmy Lou marry. That night, the giant Emmy Lou is lying under the stars and plaintively asks Artie if he still loves her; Costello plays this beautifully, assuring her of his undying devotion. This lovely scene is followed by some good bits of business as Emmy Lou tries to fix breakfast with some very small utensils. Emmy is famished herself, so Artie convinces Raven (along with some townspeople played by veteran comic actors Charles Lane, Doodles Weaver, Herbie Faye and Bobby Barber) to help out. In a funny ex-change, one admits he never had to prepare a ninety-foot hotdog, while the other laments "I had to get the bun!"

In a futile attempt to keep everyone out of sight, Raven gives Artie and Emmy Lou a new house—rather, a remote barn. As Emmy is feeling both slighted and soiled, Artie, with a big hose, gives her a shower—which causes her to grow even more. Her size attracts the attention of the Army, who immediately assume she is an alien presence. Artie and Emmy Lou's more immediate problem is her growing resentment with everyone, including the newly prominent Artie (Raven has given him cars and "titles" to hush everything up). In 1957, Provine had played gangster Bonnie Parker in *The Bonnie Parker Story*; the threatening rage she displayed there is put to good use as Emmy Lou comes to town, ridicules, then douses water on the cowering townspeople, uproots some of Raven's beloved trees, and sends the top of the tower on a spin that makes it appear to be a flying saucer.

As the Army gears up to battle this "alien creature," a contrite Emmy Lou turns to Artie (and Max) to save her. What results is a protracted and unfunny climax wherein Artie gets Max to do some time tampering, causing Artie and the inept soldiers to don Civil War attire, then Napoleonic garb, then prehistoric outfits. It comes off as gratuitous,

especially when Max finally brings her back to normal by "himself." All ends happily when the Army realizes the power of Max and the brilliance of Artie, which makes Artie the new "big man" in town and relegates Raven to has-been status in everyone's eyes. A grateful, normal-sized Emmy Lou walks alongside her recognized hubby, and in a final good visual, Artie's dog Corporal, now giant-size, trails behind.

Lou Costello never lived to see the film's release in August 1959, as he died in March of that year. That may be why there has been a bit of a pall cast on this fairly good-natured film. *The 30 Foot Bride of Candy Rock* is certainly not flawless; it isn't even particularly funny. It is a good showcase for Dorothy Provine, and a final reminder that Costello was not only a skilled comedian but a pretty decent actor as well, one who could touch the heart as well as the funny bone.

1959

JUSTIN HUMPHREYS

If you see American International Pictures' logo on a movie made between roughly 1957 and 1977, you are 99% guaranteed of being entertained. *Attack of the Giant Leeches* (or *The Giant Leeches*, as its ads touted it) is a kind of companion piece to AIP's *Night of the Blood Beast*. *Attack of the Giant Leeches* epitomizes the kind of inexpensive, lively, and endlessly rewatchable meat-and-potatoes drive-in monster fare that AIP excelled at in their early years. Is it, by any critical standard, an outstanding film? No. Would I watch it twenty times before revisiting a dull Oscar movie like *The English Patient* even once? A resounding YES!

If Erskine Caldwell wrote a drive-in horror movie, it would go something like *Attack of the Giant Leeches*; he might have called it *God's Little Quagmire*. The cornpone atmosphere is thick here, like in other swamp-based drive-in champs like 1957's *Bayou*. About all it lacks in being a *Snuffy Smith* comic strip is hills and moonshine jugs with "XXX" scrawled on them. Set in the Florida Everglades, man-sized mutant leeches wipe out the wildlife in their vicinity, then work up to draining the local hayseeds' blood. Game Warden Steve Benton (Ken Clark) investigates the murders, while his girlfriend Nan's

(Jan Shepard) dad, Doc Greyson (Tyler McVey) tries to coax him into fishing with dynamite to shake the creatures loose.

Meanwhile, dry goods storeowner Dave Walker (the great Bruno Ve Sota) catches his slutty Daisy Mae wife, Liz (Yvette Vickers), in *flagrante delicto* with his pal, Cal (Michael Emmet), and drives them at gunpoint into the bog, and unwittingly into the leeches' eager suckers. In the last reel, the rustics band together to exterminate these unwelcome critters, and a cockamamie, tacked-on bit of dialogue provides some vague explanation for their existence: "Maybe the proximity of Cape Canaveral's got something to do with it!", Doc Greyson suggests.

Attack of the Giant Leeches is a kind of companion piece to AIP's *Night of the Blood Beast*. Both were directed by Bernard L. Kowalski, have the same strident, radio show-like musical scores, and feature actor Ross Sturlin as a monster. The definition of a journeyman, Kowalski was an unexceptional filmmaker who mainly worked in TV. His later credits include *Krakatoa, East of Java* (1968), the bloody western *Macho Callahan* (1970), and a return to drive-in horror form with *Sssssss* (1973). *Giant Leeches* and *Blood Beast* remain two of his most entertaining productions, and are surprisingly professional pieces of filmmaking for movies that cost about two dollars and change. And since they were produced by the Corman brothers, Gene and Roger, that's about *all* they cost.

The film's crew is dotted with Corman mainstays like art director Daniel Haller, so you know every expense will be spared, but the gifted Haller will still make it look respectable. The cast includes welcome familiar faces like prolific B-movie fixture Gene Roth, doing the kind of lame, all-purpose Southern accent that Hollywood stars *still* perpetrate (Note his half-assed "Southern" pronunciation of "guarantee").

Most notably, though, there's pinup queen Yvette Vickers. As a bad girl akin to the one she played in *Attack of the 50-Foot Woman* (see earlier chapter), Vickers looks like she stepped off the cover of an exceptionally sordid pulp paperback (At one point, Ve Sota calls her a "she-cat"; characters speaking what sounds like purple movie trailer narration makes any movie better). Vickers outlives the leeches' other captives in their underwater lair, undoubtedly as an excuse for the camera to linger on her bare legs as long as possible.

Along with Vickers, the real star is Ve Sota. I actively like almost every movie he was ever involved in, except for 1962's godawful *Invasion of the Star Creatures*, which he directed. The rotund Ve Sota's run with Roger Corman was long and rich, with him showing up in character roles in *Rock All Night*, *A Bucket of Blood*, *The Haunted Palace*, *The Undead*, *ad infinitum*. And aside from '50's-'60's gems like those, his "B"-movie credentials are sterling, from his cameo in *Night Tide* (1961), which was distributed by Corman, to his unforgettable silent performance as the wealthy, gluttonous lech in 1955's *Dementia* (a.k.a. *Daughter of Horror*). Like his peer, Dick Miller, Ve Sota is a welcome presence in anything. As a director, he made the watchable *The Brain Eaters* (1958) and claimed to have co-directed *Dementia*, which is a must-see little marvel.

Despite the leech costumes' silliness, there's something surreal and vaguely unsettling about cheapjack creature f/x like these that money and polish can't replicate. They remind me of something *Basket Case* director Frank Henenlotter said about Paul Blaisdell's madly inventive 1950's monster suits for AIP: They may look ridiculous in a movie, but imagine one creeping toward you in a dark alley at midnight. An L.A. native I know recalls seeing the film as a kid on local TV and being terrified by the eyeless, faceless creatures.

The beasts here look something like a cross between real leeches and barnacles, but more like a starfish's tentacles. Their burbling, pulsating, biomechanical sounds are much more effective than their patchwork raincoat costumes. There's practically no rhyme or reason to their physicality in or out of the bayou—it's just a case of the two performers (Sturlin and Guy Buccola, both uncredited) donning the bizarre suits, jumping in the water, and moving around. As previously mentioned, in 1958, Sturlin had played Kowalski's Blood Beast, and that same year—since Corman perpetually recycled everything—he later climbed back into the Blood Beast suit as the "Outsider", a faux monster spooking primitive, post-apocalyptic folk in Corman's *Teenage Caveman*.

Most of *Giant Leeches*' exteriors were shot at the Arboretum in Arcadia, California, a gorgeous botanical garden and ubiquitous movie location that pops up in everything from Preston Sturges' *The Lady Eve* to Bert I. Gordon's *The Cyclops* (see earlier chapter). The original *Fantasy Island* opens with Herve Villechaize hollering "The plane! The plane!" from the Arboretum's Queen Anne cottage. Like Bronson Canyon, the Arboretum's grounds have represented nearly every conceivable place on earth onscreen, and, luckily, it's still very recognizable, and almost certainly leech-free.

As for *Giant Leeches'* overall look, I'm convinced that some movies actually come off better — or at least more moodily — on VHS than DVD or BluRay. There's something about that medium's shoddiness that enhances certain films' sordid atmosphere. The old Thorn-EMI VHS of *Dawn of the Dead* or the Columbia tape of *Taxi Driver* capture those movies' rancidness with greater fidelity than their sharp, crisp BluRay versions. *The Giant Leeches* VHS that I grew-up watching was from Sinister Cinema, a venerable supplier of rare titles. That Sinister's release was a second-rate transfer apparently made from a fairly ratty 16mm print suited the movies' dark, muddy milieu very nicely. It made the smudged glass of the tank Kowalski filmed his underwater scenes in look even stranger and gauzier; likewise, the cheaply creepy, chiaroscuro lighting in the leeches' hideaway.

But no matter how sharp or greasy *Attack of the Giant Leeches* looks, or how weirdly appealing the leeches themselves are, there's no getting around it being another example of there never having been an outstanding leech-centric horror movie. That seems odd, since their intrinsic repulsiveness for the average viewer makes them seemingly ideal monster movie fodder. But whether they're in a Universal "B" picture like *The Leech Woman* (1960) or straight-to-video junk like *Leeches!* (2003), they seem to only inspire pulp. To produce a truly skin-crawling effect, leeches come off best in their natural form—the way that people can most closely relate to them and their odious workings - like in *The African Queen* or *Stand By Me*. The moral of this story seems to be that, in some matters - like monsters - size doesn't count for much.

1961

MIKE PEROS

My fated path to *Konga* began several years ago, when I watched *Horrors of the Black Museum* (1957) for the first time. Produced and written by Herman Cohen, it's about a series of murders rocking London, with Michael Gough as a reporter taking the British bobbies to task for not catching the killer. This character was arrogant, abrasive, quick to anger, but I thought he was on the side of law and order—until we found out otherwise. I wouldn't have been surprised had I known the oeuvre of the emotional juggernaut that is Michael Gough. I had seen him in *Horror of Dracula* (1958) but he couldn't compete with Christopher Lee's Count. Here, however, whether lacing into the police, taunting men and women alike, and exploding on a whim, I found Gough fascinating. You never knew — and always looked forward to — when he would "lose it." It could be mid-paragraph, mid-sentence ("What do you MEAN BY THIS!!!??"), even mid-word.

I had to seek out more Gough and found that he and American writer/producer Herman Cohen joined forces on five films from the late 1950's through 1970, all written by Cohen and each (but for one) tailored to Gough's particular gifts, but the first three efforts with Cohen are the ones that yield Gough cinematic gold. Besides *Horrors of the Black*

Museum, there was 1963's *The Black Zoo*, a loose reworking of 1933's *Murders in the Zoo*, wherein Gough's maniacal zookeeper will do anything to save his zoo, including using animals to kill his enemies. The movie also portrays a deeply twisted relationship between Gough and his bitter wife. Their squabbles are filled with such vitriol that they would give *Who's Afraid of Virginia Woolf*'s George and Martha a run for their money.

However, it's the 1961 Cohen/Gough collaboration *Konga*, directed by John Lemont, that is the apex of Gough's career. If one wants to see the essence of Gough in one film, this is it. *Konga* begins with Gough's Professor Decker arriving in London after having been presumed dead for a year when his plane crashed in Africa. He has spent time among the natives in Uganda, and has brought home his pet chimp, Konga, to whom he is devoted, and vice-versa. Interviewed by reporters, Gough's Decker is relaxed and confident that his findings on insectivorous plants and a new link between "what grows in the earth and animal life" will revolutionize science. When Decker gets home, he's not as charming with long-suffering assistant, Margaret (Margo Johns). She is quite perturbed when he shows more affection to Konga than to her. Not even bothering to placate her, Decker then proceeds to the greenhouse, where he ferociously yanks out all the flowers and raises the temperature to a sweltering ninety degrees to accommodate the carnivorous plants he has brought over. If that isn't enough to make Margaret wish to be traded from "Team Gough," he then shoots her cat Tabby after it starts lapping up some spilled serum, dying before any reaction can occur.

Nevertheless Margaret, in the cause of science and an inexplicable infatuation with Gough's Decker (when you watch the film, you'll see he never reciprocates her affections, and the one time she kisses him, he disgustedly wipes it off), remains to see these plants' accelerated growth within a week. (Many are black and resemble discarded models for Audrey from *Little Shop of Horrors*.) Gough uses the serum, augmented with seeds that make the subject subservient, on Konga and lo and behold, this cuddly little chimp instantly morphs into a hulking…gorilla. (It's actually an actor named Paul Stockman in a gorilla suit.)

This added bulk on Konga will later prove useful to Decker after he meets with the angry college dean, who condemns Decker's assertions. This scene between Gough and the dean is archetypal Gough: displaying a seething calm which escalates rapidly, especially after the dean suggests he's mad. "NO one will STOP ME!" Decker exclaims—and he should have believed him, because later that same night, Decker orders Konga to strangle him. Margaret is critical yet forgiving—but she makes it clear that marriage is the price for her silence. Gough smilingly defers in such an unctuous manner that any marriage-minded woman possessing a trace of her faculties would have seen through it—I guess love is blind.

The police interview Decker, who admits to a scientific disagreement with the dean—and the detectives let it go at that. That evening, a scientific rival appears at Decker's party and admits he too has discovered a mutation that will accelerate growth. When this scientist allows Decker to see his research later that night and foolishly says, "Knock hard as I have no servants," Decker has the chance to use Konga again. After a brief meeting, Gough telegraphs his intentions (at least, to the viewer), then proclaims, "I have earned the glory that is mine. Professor… you are TOO LATE!" Wherein, Konga dramatically appears and puts a violent end to the professor.

Margaret again forgives and forgets while the police are still mystified, even though there is a connection between Decker, the dead dean, and the perishable professor. And Gough's Decker repays her loyalty by so overtly chasing his comely young student, Sondra (Claire Gordon), that her classmates can't help but needle Sondra's brooding boyfriend, Bob (Jess Conrad), during a field trip. When Bob demands that Decker leave Sondra alone, we get another Gough eruption ("ARE you THREAT -en-ing ME-E-E??") followed by some grappling, after which Bob and Gough appear to make tentative amends. However, Gough can't let things go, and Konga dutifully kills Bob right in front of his parents' house.

You would think the police might have zeroed in on Decker, since they have found similar hairs, like that of a chimpanzee, on all three victims. But no, which brings us to the over-the-top final fifteen minutes. Margaret warns Decker about the police, which he brushes off, hinting he may dispose of Konga. He then invites Sondra to dinner and takes her to the greenhouse—while Margaret observes from the outside. In classic Gough fashion, he segues from a desire to have Sondra's mind to his primal urge to have her body: "I need you to BE WITH ME!" As he is groping Sondra, Margaret plies Konga with an ultra-heavy dose of the serum. Instantly, Konga grows bigger than a house, sets the greenhouse, as well as Margaret, ablaze, and grabs Gough for an old-fashioned walk through London-town. This proves quite amusing thanks to the close-ups of Gough writhing and yelling "Put me down!" However, Konga's stroll (carrying a Gough doll) is a bit of a letdown, since he actually does very little damage (it must be that famous British reserve), aside from a few tentative grabs at the scurrying people below (He does hurl Gough to the pavement, but that's understandable). Finally, the police and army join forces and take Konga down, at which point the dying Konga reverts to his little chimp self, alongside his master who done him wrong.

Konga may not win any awards, but it's entertaining no matter how many times you've seen it, mainly because of Gough. While he has given many enjoyable, and even subtle, performances in dozens of films (he is certainly best known globally as Alfred in the Burton/Schumacher *Batman* films), this is one of the few chances for him to display all the weapons in his histrionic arsenal. One sees the highs, the lows, and the smarmy calm in between. All of Gough's characters in the horror genre are maniacally self-absorbed, so it's only fitting that in the end, his most meaningful human interaction is with a chimpanzee.

1962

LARRY BLAMIRE

When Tim Lucas invited me to record a segment on his commentary track for the Blu-ray release of *The Magic Sword*, I was (like the movie's Siamese twins) beside myself. Kino Lorber's Blu-ray was stunning, rewarding our patience during years of upgrades. *The Magic Sword* finally received its due. Has a budget so low ever looked so glorious? When I met its director, Bert I. Gordon (deservedly well-represented in this volume), I was happy to tell him that I felt *The Magic Sword* was not only his best film, but one of my all-time favorites, and that the ingenuity he employed was somewhat miraculous.

For me, it's one of those rare films whose glow has not faded since I was a wee lad. I focused on what I call "the Six," that being the six great quest films in the fantasy wave of the late 50's/early 60's: *The 7th Voyage of Sinbad* (1958), the Steve Reeves *Thief of Bagdad* (1961), *Jack the Giant Killer* and *The Magic Sword* (both 1962), *Captain Sindbad* and *Jason and the Argonauts* (both 1963). *The Magic Sword* is probably the darkest.

The Magic Sword's grand opening credits scream classic Hollywood (you know you're about to see A MOVIE). We are instantly transported by Richard Markowitz's dignified, heroic, elegiac main title theme, and I cannot overstate the composer's contribution to the movie's success. The film quickly introduces hero George (Gary Lockwood), Princess

Helene (Anne Helm) whom he worships from afar, batty sorceress step-mom Sybil (Estelle Winwood), Helene's dad/king (Merritt Stone) and arrogant suitor Sir Branton (Liam Sullivan). Into this mix comes (cue thunder and lightning) wicked sorcerer Lodac (Basil Rathbone), who kidnaps Helene to avenge his sister's death, psyched to feed her to his pet dragon in seven days. Seven times does he curse the road to his castle, because… what is a quest without obstacles? The conniving Branton vows to get her back and win her hand.

Watching all this in Sybil's magic pool, George tricks Mom, seals her in a basement and commandeers the nifty magical gifts promised for his twenty-first birthday: the magical steed Bayard, invulnerable armor, and the title sword itself, Ascalon the Blade. He also frees six brave knights, long petrified, who vow to aid in his quest.

Our first unsettling moment is at a garden pool when Helene is kidnapped while bathing. A creepy echoic voice calls her name, and a ghostly transparent woman glides toward her. This is the only time we see Maila Nurmi (the iconic Vampira herself) when she's not beneath the hag mask. The apparition abruptly freezes and her eyes glow; a deliciously alarming scene for a young Monster Kid.

The first of Ladoc's curses was always my favorite. The lead-up is dark and moody as the knights ride through a forbidding forest of grim, twisted trees against black sky; the studio unnaturalness working in its favor. The ogre's presence is foretold by several heavy booms, which turn out to be massive logs being hurled. The monster is an interesting creation: actor Jack Kosslyn under tattered clothes, thick tufts of hair and hideous prosthetic makeup. The obvious mask does little to diminish his fearsome bearing. His arms are partly restricted, lending an odd physicality, while the limited mobility dictated by the process shot setup forces the knights to essentially bring the battle to *him*. Though potentially static, this peculiar staging works, and (two slain knights later) George decides to literally run rings around the giant via his magic steed. Composer Markowitz introduces a relentless "jabbing motif" he will later return to, then a delirious orchestral onslaught that conveys the horse's mounting speed and the ogre's increasing dizziness. When the beast collapses to his knees, George runs him through, accompanied by a powerful organ cue, representative of the sword.

The next curse up is the swamp that dissolves Sir Anthony (one of the six freed knights) down to a skeleton and while it suggests acid, given that he struggles for a while, the movie prefers we chalk it up to dark magic. George himself is lifted from its bubbling death by his blade. But my favorite part is the quiet lead-in as the heroes slowly make their way through a fog-choked studio swamp nightmare world. For much of it, Markowitz goes minimal with a soft, two-note drumbeat that is faintly unnerving as knights call out for their missing companion.

The mill sequence contains some of Gordon's best direction. As Rathbone's Lodac and the double-crossing Branton conspire inside (a wonderful example of the script's sharp wit, courtesy of Gordon and Bernard C. Schoenfeld), outside, a suspicious Sir Dennis (Jacques Gallo) approaches the mill (and the camera). A lovely French farm girl (Danielle De Metz) crosses frame behind him, carrying a basket, singing *Frère Jacques*. It is to Gordon's credit that he confidently lets their encounter live in French, sans subtitles, making their transition to playful lovemaking all the more genuine and understated. Which plays perfectly into the shocking reveal, as Dennis pulls back to find he's kissing Maila Nurmi's hag. Let me tell you, it doesn't matter that it's a mask, it's still a lovely piece of pop-eyed grotesquerie (it scarred my little brother for years). Her vampiric attack (right on the neck, with blood) is thwarted by the cross on George's shield as he arrives just in time. For her failure, the hag is scolded by Lodac, and Nurmi's pathetic, querulous whining is wonderful.

The fate of Sirs Dennis and James (Angus Duncan) has to be one of the grimmest in kiddie matinee history, and its impact is only heightened by its indefinability. As in: what the hell is that intense spiral up on the mountain roasting them alive? At its mercy, the two painfully turn and walk towards camera, hair and tunics burned off, skin scorched, only to fade from existence as they try to warn George and Patrick. The reasoning that they were disintegrated by heat does not lessen its existential horror.

The cavern of evil spirits (our old pal, Bronson Caves for exteriors) is a nice exercise in neatly building dread as George and the Irish Sir Patrick (John Mauldin) search for a way out. Fleeting glimpses and sounds gradually increase until ghoulish phantom heads float towards them, their high-pitched wails reminiscent of the icy strings in

Penderecki's Awakening of Jacob (employed by Kubrick in *The Shining*). Patrick, possessed by one, still manages to free George, using what Lodac sneeringly refers to as "the power of Patrick's faith."

Throughout the quest, we have cut to Helene's terrifying experiences at Lodac's castle, a colorfully macabre domain of assorted minions—some blue-skinned, some with bird heads—who at one point join in a feast presided over by Nurmi's fussing hag. And true to Gordon's nickname of "Mr. B.I.G.", there's a cage full of tiny people, crucial to the climax, allowing for some dandy outsized props, including a perfect version of George's sword.

When the dragon finally appears, my son Griffin (12 as of this writing) declared it the finest he'd seen. Truly, there's much majesty in its CG-free solidity. I cannot express my joy when Griff immediately fell in love with this movie just as I had. He's probably watched it more than me. It gives me hope.

As to cast, the underrated Gary Lockwood (see Gene Roddenberry's first series *The Lieutenant*) is earnest and grounded as George, and Anne Helm equally convincing. Estelle Winwood is an eccentric treasure, Liam Sullivan as dryly amusing as he is odious. Best of all is Rathbone in what seems a culmination of his great swashbuckling villains; vigorous, rapier-sharp, snapping off snide remarks. Of the knights, Gallo's Dennis and Mauldin's Patrick are the standouts.

In fact, Sir Patrick is Griffin's favorite, and he does a spot-on impression. Even made himself an Irish shield out of cardboard. And he was most pleased that in the end, the slain knights, like the movie itself, live on.

1962/1964

BRIAN R. SOLOMON

It's a shame that *Gorath* isn't more widely available in domestic markets today, because to see this movie is to take in the majesty of Toho Studio at the absolute zenith of its powers, during a boom in special effects ("*tokusatsu*") movies that stretched for roughly a decade from the late 50's to the late 60's. It's a highly influential movie that would have later impact on disaster movies that include most notably *Armageddon* (1998), which copied several elements. It also showcases the brilliant work of Toho effects master Eiji Tsuburaya to an unparalleled degree, particularly the staggering model work for which he was famous.

The ironic thing about the film is that while it does boast a giant beast — one of the most bizarre and unforgettable ever seen, in fact — that's only a small component of the film. There's so much more to recommend it than the brief appearance of the giant walrus/lizard later christened "Maguma". The wide-screen TohoScope aspect ratio, the brilliant color, and an ensemble cast of several dependable Toho regulars make *Gorath* a masterpiece of the genre, one that is begging for an international release in English.

Released in Japan in March 1962 as *Yosei Gorasu* (translated as either *Ominous Star Gorath* or *Calamity Star Gorath*), the film takes place in what was then the future of the late 70's and early 80's, when a massive rogue star, the movie's titular menace, is hurtling towards Earth with a gravitational pull that spells certain destruction unless a solution is found. That solution comes in the form of an international cooperative spearheaded by Japan, in which rather than attempt to destroy Gorath or shift its trajectory, the actual orbit of the Earth will be slightly altered to avoid the impact. To accomplish this, a massive network of thrusters is constructed at the South Pole, with a degree of quickness that stretches the limits of plausibility—although this is a movie with a giant walrus in it, so everything is relative.

And speaking of the giant walrus in question, in what is admittedly the film's most ludicrous moment, the beast is awakened thanks to the cavern excavations going on at the South Pole during the construction of those thrusters, and the movie pauses its entire plot to showcase the monster's attack, and the military strike against it, in which laser weapons are eventually used to kill it. If you watch the movie and think that the whole sequence feels strangely out of place, you're not the only one. Director Ishiro Honda fought against it, but Toho Executive Producer Tomoyuki Tanaka insisted that a giant monster, or *kaiju*, needed to be included, and Honda eventually caved in to his demands, much to his later regret. Interestingly, the Maguma sequence would later be largely removed for the 1964 American release of the film, precisely because test audiences and distributors—who jokingly dubbed the creature "Wally the Walrus"—found the whole thing too ridiculous to take seriously in an otherwise very sober disaster epic.

But all that aside, what works in the film far outweighs what doesn't. The script by serious science fiction screenwriter Takeshi Kimura, who had previously penned such Toho classics as *Rodan* (1956), *The Mysterians* (1957), *The H-Man* (1958) and *The Human Vapor* (1960), is filled with moments of real gravitas and poignancy not always seen in the more whimsical *tokusatsu* efforts of the 1960's, giving the actors a lot of meat on the bone and allowing them an impressive emotional range. These include *tokusatsu* vets like Ryo Ikebe (*Battle in Outer Space*, 1959) as astrophysicist Dr. Tazawa; young and handsome Akira Kubo, who would later be seen in a string of *Showa-era* Godzilla films, as an astronaut on a fact-finding mission to intercept Gorath; and the beautiful Kumi Mizuno, best known as Namikawa in *Invasion of Astro Monster* (1964), as the astronaut's devoted and put-upon girlfriend. Add

Toho all-stars such as Kenji Sahara, Akihiko Hirata and the venerable Takashi Shimura, and you have one of the most impressive Toho ensemble casts ever put together.

Although the special effects work of Toho, and Japanese *tokusatsu* cinema in general, has often been snarkily derided in later years, that's a very unfair assessment. It's of major importance to remember that at the time, particularly in the late 50's and well into the 1960's, the effects work of the Tsuburaya unit at Toho was not only on the cutting edge, but doing some of the finest work anywhere in the industry, and anywhere in the world. These were treated as A-pictures, with sizable budgets and impressive resources, and all you have to do is take a look at the science fiction B-movie output coming from Hollywood in the same era to realize that Toho was actually leading the industry at the time. Few movies showcase this better than *Gorath*.

Nevertheless, it might have been the lack of an effective giant monster subplot that hamstrung the movie in the United States. By 1964, American audiences were accustomed to getting giant monsters in their Japanese releases, and this more cerebral effort failed to really connect with audiences. The re-edited version, minus the walrus, but with an added introduction from ubiquitous voiceover artist Paul Frees to help explain the science-heavy plot for 60's viewers not yet accustomed to such storylines, was released in California in May 1964 as part of a double-bill with *The Human Vapor* (another Honda-Kimura collaboration), but failed to make back the money the American distributor (Brenco Pictures) had laid out to acquire it, contributing to the demise of the company a short time later. A later version would eventually be seen on American television, shortened even further and with the introduction removed.

It's that chopped-up American TV version that later made its way to VHS in the 80's, but aside from that, the film has been largely unavailable in the United States. No official release of the original Japanese version, in English or any other language, has ever been made available in the United States on DVD or Blu-Ray, although the film has been known to pop up now and then on streaming channel Comet TV, a special treat for vigilant fans. It was recently given the deluxe treatment by Toho as part of a Japanese home video release packaged with other studio classics like *Varan* (1958), *Dogora* (1964) and *Space Amoeba* (1970).

Although one of the lesser-known Toho projects, *Gorath* has gotten some love over the years. The giant star, reimagined as an asteroid, does appear in the 2004 monster rally *Godzilla: Final Wars*. And even Maguma has been known to pop up in various Godzilla video games and other Toho promotional material over the years.

Yes, there are science anomalies galore. How could a massive star with intense gravitational pull get close enough to Earth to destroy the moon yet cause little more damage to Earth than some unusual tidal activity? The questions of how the Earth will be returned to its normal orbit and what the altered orbit will do to the planet are left open-ended at the end of the movie. But unless you're the kind of stickler who lets things like this bother you, *Gorath* is an extremely entertaining and impressive science fiction epic from a studio responsible for some of the finest genre entries seen before the rise of Lucasfilm. Come for the giant walrus-reptile attack, stay for the international intrigue, gorgeous production design, and ingenuous practical effects.

Jack the Giant Killer

1962

TRACY MERCER

The Fates — with more than a little help from the power players behind this publication — provided me with this opportunity to discuss 1962's *Jack the Giant Killer*. Imagine my surprise viewing this film immediately after watching 1958's *The 7th Voyage of Sinbad* (which I also write about in this book) AND feeling like I was seeing double!

Follow: Both films are directed by Nathan Juran. Both films star the gorgeous/wooden Kerwin Mathews as the dashing hero. Both films cast Torin Thatcher as the bad guy with magical powers. Both films are set in far-off places and revolve around a hero's journey fighting fantastical monsters and evil forces in order to save a princess from grave harm. One film has a magic lamp with an enslaved genie who can help save our protagonists by granting wishes even as he really seeks to be freed from his prison of a lamp. One film has an enslaved leprechaun who can help save our protagonists by granting wishes even as he really seeks to be freed from his prison of a glass bottle. Oh, and both movies employ stop-motion special effects to bring creatures to dazzling, celluloid life.

The biggest difference is that Ray Harryhausen has nothing to do with *Jack the Giant Killer* though the filmmakers here flatter his work by mightily trying to imitate it.

I'm not a copyright lawyer, but I can certainly understand why Columbia Pictures initially threatened to sue *Jack the Giant Killer*'s producer, Edward Small, and his distributor, United Artists.

The striking similarities between *The 7th Voyage of Sinbad* and *Jack the Giant Killer* reminded me of a similar filmic déjà vu experience I've only had once before. Growing up with cinephile parents who indoctrinated me to the James Bond franchise, I was always a fan of 1965's *Thunderball*. What's not to love about Sean Connery as Bond and a very simple plot about Bond having to find two atomic bombs stolen by SPECTRE before they can be put to use? Cut to 1983. Sean Connery returns to his signature role in *Never Say Never Again*. The Plot? Bond must find two nuclear weapons stolen by SPECTRE before they can be put to use. BUT in the case of the two Bond films, *Never Say Never Again* literally IS a remake of *Thunderball* due to a legal victory of writers Kevin McClory and Jack Whittingham who, with Ian Fleming, wrote a story that became the basis for Fleming's novel, *Thunderball*.

But how to explain *Jack the Giant Killer*'s eerily similar story to *Sinbad*? Funnily enough, producer Edward Small saw *The 7th Voyage of Sinbad*'s box office success and decided to make his own film in a similar vein. This becomes extra amusing once you learn that Ray Harryhausen had tried to approach Small to help produce his *Sinbad* years earlier but could not get past his gatekeepers. By design, Small tried to re-create Harryhausen's triumph right down to casting his two leads and bringing on the same director. I'm grateful for Small's efforts that led to this absolutely delightful, action-driven film. Also fun: Jack has a bigger body count and smartly sustains an air of danger and violence throughout which stands in contrast to the 'softer,' more dreamlike treatment of *The 7th Voyage of Sinbad*'s similar story.

If Harryhausen's *Sinbad* played fast and loose with Greek mythology, the same can also be said for Small's take on the Cornish folklore tale of *Jack the Giant Killer*. The original fable tells the story of a farmer who had adventures in the time of King Arthur that thrust him into conflict with a spectrum of giants who he excelled at slaying. In fact, he was so good at being a giant killer, he was granted a seat at Arthur's Round Table. By contrast, in Small's 1962 film, there is an exposition-heavy opening that outlines our story essentials: An evil sorcerer named Pendragon, who is also known as The Black Prince, tried to use his command of creatures, including hobgoblins, giants, and witches to take over the kingdom of Cornwall. Only a wickedly powerful and savvy wizard named Herla saved the day by using his powers to trap Pendragon and his enablers in exile. Plotting his return to Cornwall with the goal of ruling the kingdom is Pendragon's reason for living, and becomes reality after Herla dies.

The film quickly introduces us to the daughter of King Mark of Cornwall, the gorgeous Princess Elaine (Judi Meredith). Pendragon, passing himself off as a foreign Lord named Elidoras, gifts the Princess a creepy music box with an even creepier mini dancing jester who would totally be at home in Charles Band's *Puppet Master* franchise. The jester waits for the Princess to fall asleep before turning into giant named Cormoran who abducts the princess and escapes the castle. While attempting to put the Princess on Pendragon's ship, the giant Cormoran is slain by a local farmer named Jack (Kerwin Mathews). That's it. That's the only giant we ever see Jack slay in this 94-minute film.

Grateful for the safe return of his daughter, the King of Cornwall knights farmer Jack and essentially makes him the Kevin Costner Bodyguard to Elaine's Whitney Houston. And just like that 90's film, our two leads fall for each other even while trying to dodge mortal threats. The king, without buy-in from his daughter, decides that Pendragon poses too big a threat to Princess Elaine and charges Jack with getting her to a convent across the sea, where she will be safe. A successful extraction of Elaine from Jack's care by howling demon witches give Pendragon the upper hand. He demands the king abdicate within a week so Pendragon can become the new king with his Queen-to-be, Elaine by his side, or else he will kill her.

Jack, with Peter — a young son of the murdered Captain of the ship the witches attacked — are rescued by a Viking named Sigurd who just happens to own an imprisoned leprechaun in a bottle. The leprechaun explains that if you are pure of heart, he has three golden coins that can be used to grant wishes. Seeking freedom, the leprechaun agrees to help Jack save the princess from Pendragon's clutches in exchange for being set free, and thus, our ragtag crew is transported to Pendragon's castle.

Plot twist: When Elaine can't touch the leprechaun's bottle without burning her hand, it becomes clear that Pendragon has Elaine under his dark spell. This allows her to easily drug Jack with a sleeping potion and we see Pendragon turn little Peter into a chimpanzee and Sigurd into a dog. Jack, smashing Elaine's mirror, somehow breaks the dark spell, turning Elaine back to her normal, not-possessed self.

Fleeing the castle, Jack and friends are saved from Pendragon's animated, two-headed giant by having the leprechaun conjure a sea monster who slays the giant. Jack, Elaine, Peter, and Sigurd make it to a ship only to see Jack forced into a climactic battle with Pendragon, who has taken the form of a winged harpy! Once Pendragon is slain, his castle crumbles, killing his minions, and Jack frees the leprechaun as promised. Peter and Sigurd are returned back to their normal human forms. The leprechaun heads back to Ireland free and even creates an Oz-like rainbow to help guide our victorious heroes back to Cornwall. Maybe they will meet Sinbad and his princess along the way? Now that would be a terrific cinematic crossover I'd love to see!

1962/1963

TRACY MERCER

When we talk about *King Kong vs. Godzilla,* we have to celebrate just how many "firsts" are associated with this Toho classic that brought "East meets West" magnificent beasts together. A licensing deal between RKO and Toho allowed film fans to see King Kong back top-lining theater marquees for the first time since the 1933 rushed-sequel to *King Kong, The Son of Kong* (see opening chapters on both films). It also represents the first time either King Kong or Godzilla were seen battling while filling up a wide screen, and it's the first time we saw either creature in color! Upon its initial release, *King Kong vs. Godzilla* became the then second highest grossing film in Japanese history, super-charging the cycle of Toho Godzilla films to come. While today, we may be used to seeing beloved screen creatures with their own franchises paired up — with titles like *Alien vs Predator* and *Jason vs Freddy* immediately coming to mind — but back in 1962, that wasn't a trend (1943's *Frankenstein Meets The Wolf Man* notwithstanding).

As detailed in our opening chapter, the character of King Kong was the brainchild of American filmmaker, Merian C. Cooper. The 1933 film tells the story of Kong being found by a film crew on Skull Island somewhere in the Indian Ocean. Kong falls in love with a beautiful actress who is with the crew — played by the stunning Fay Wray. The crew then takes the majestic beast from his island home to New York where they market him as an amusement to see, dubbing him "The Eighth Wonder of the World." Eventually Kong breaks free, only to fatefully climb the Empire State Building to protect his favorite blonde actress before he is brutally shot by a phalanx of biplanes armed with gatling guns. Brutally shot up, Kong falls to earth and dies. If you have a heart, it's impossible to watch the film's climax and not tear up and shake your head when we are told, "It wasn't the airplanes. It was beauty killed the beast."

In 1991, *King Kong* was inducted into the US Library of Congress by being selected for preservation in the National Film Registry because it was deemed "culturally, historically and aesthetically significant." A large part of that significance is the groundbreaking visual effects work of Willis Harold O'Brien, also known for his work on *The Lost World*, *The Last Days of Pompeii*, and *Mighty Joe Young*, for which he won an Oscar for Best Visual Effects. By contrast, no one will ever say the "guy in a gorilla suit" for *King Kong vs. Godzilla* can hold a candle to O'Brien's elegant stop-motion work done 30 years prior. In fact, a friend astutely suggested the Toho Kong looks drunk. BUT, there is a connection between O'Brien and the 1962 film to red flag. Originally, O'Brien had conceived of a *King Kong vs. Frankenstein* (monster) concept. He even wrote a story treatment and generated concept art. He was introduced to producer John Beck who hired George Worthing Yates (*It Came from Beneath the Sea* and *War of the Colossal Beast*, both reviewed in this book) to write a script based on O'Brien's story. Not finding a home in the states, Beck, without O'Brien's knowledge, shopped the script to Toho. Toho removed Frankenstein's monster as a concept and inserted Godzilla once RKO gave Toho permission for the use of Kong. O'Brien was left out with no money or credit for his idea that anchored the 1962 film.

While there is scant character development in director Ishiro Honda's film, it's because the filmmaker (who's got a whopping seven films discussed in this book!) understood the assignment: let's see Kong and Godzilla duke it out in epic battles! That being said, there are threads of savvy dark humor and political overtones that help drive the plot until we get to the monsters. Genre films can be terrific delivery vehicles for social commentary and the cartoonish portrayal of a media hungry, Big Pharma-forward doctor still feels very current. Further, with global warming impacting our climate with seemingly greater devastation each year, the melting of the iceberg and the heating up of the Arctic that unleashes Godzilla plays like a current metaphor for the threat our changing climate poses to our world's survival.

The film's summary below is for the 1963 American version of the film which is more readily available to watch and best known to Monster Kids. However, we should note that *King Kong vs Godzilla* was preceded by an all-Japanese version of the story, released in Japan in 1962. Two versions of the same film is something that was most famously done with the very first *kaiju* ("giant monster") film, *Gojira* (1954) with the inclusion of Raymond Burr into the dubbed 1956 American debut, rechristened *Godzilla, King of the Monsters*.

The movie opens foretelling Reality TV. No, really! We meet Dr. Tako (Ichiro Arishima), head of a giant pharmaceutical company, who also somehow produces a TV series called "Wonderful World" that is bottoming out in the ratings. He decides travel and adventure might help his quasi-reality show recover its audience and sends two of his on-air talent to Faro Island with a two-part mission: film the rumored-to-exist King Kong and also bring back a ton of bright red native berries that have uber magical healing powers and health benefits he can monetize. How he knows either of these things to be true is unclear. I should also point out that the racist brownface on Japanese actors playing the tribal natives could never have been a good idea.

We cut to a submarine investigating a "hot spot" in the Arctic that's giving off unexplained Geiger readings. The sub gets caught on an iceberg that contains Godzilla who is now waking up! This event is captured on TV by a rival to Dr. Tako's show. The world now knows Godzilla, a prehistoric dinosaur creature who can breathe fire, is loose and appears to be headed back to his home in Tokyo because… he just is.

Next, Kong is found on the island by Dr. Tako's crew, lead by Sakurai and Furue, drugged, and literally towed back to Tokyo. The big idea? Let's put on a televised wrestling match we can get ratings with that can capture the two beasts duking it out as they try to kill one another. It's unclear how effective human weapons will be, given explosions and poison gas don't seem to impact Godzilla. As the monsters march towards one another, we get fantastic sequences like Kong saving a small village from a ginormous octopus attack. Toho's new take on Kong has him getting more powerful with jolts of electricity! There is even a story element that calls back to Kong's love of Fay Wray's character in the 1933 original here, too — Kong seems to have a crush on Sakurai's sister, who he takes to the National Diet Building as a wink to NY's Empire State Building. Kong is effectively gassed by juice from the native berries long enough for Sakurai's sister to be taken out of harm's way. But you can't keep Kong, even one who looks drunk, down for long.

When the two beasts have their ultimate battle, it involves Godzilla's atomic breath trying to burn Kong alive while also tripping Kong and brutally slamming Kong's head with his tail. BUT when lightning hits Kong, it recharges him to full power. In the final moments, it is Kong who bests Godzilla by shoving a giant tree down his throat. The film ends with a victorious Kong heading back to the ocean so he can return to his beloved island and leave the selling of pharmaceuticals, reality TV shows, and massive Tokyo rebuilding projects, to others.

FRANKENSTEIN CONQUERS THE WORLD

1965/1966

BRIAN R. SOLOMON

The setting is a castle in Germany, near the tail end of World War II. Nazi soldiers barge in and confiscate the preserved, still-beating heart of the Frankenstein Monster from a flustered and indignant mad scientist in a strangely wordless scene. The heart is transported via top secret submarine to the Empire of Japan, where it is placed into the custody of Japanese scientists in Hiroshima. But before they can do anything with it, the city is incinerated by the infamous atomic bomb blast of August 6, 1945.

The bonkers insanity of this opening sequence sets the tone perfectly, and prepares the viewer for what is to follow, in one of the strangest and most unlikely of all giant monster movies, a Japanese and American co-production that brought one of the Western world's most iconic monsters into the Eastern world in a clash of cultures and sensibilities that produced something hard to fully explain or appreciate until you've seen it. Beloved by a cult following that includes the likes of monster movie maven Guillermo del Toro, this movie has its passionate champions and defenders, and has a development story almost as fascinating as the movie itself.

With its cycle of *tokusatsu* (special effects) and *kaiju* (giant monster) flicks in full swing, Toho Studio had taken an interest in doing something with the Frankenstein Monster, a European invention of the 19th century which had become a pop culture icon thanks to the 1930's and 40's films put out by Universal Pictures, and later the 1950's reimagining from the UK's Hammer Films. Originally, Toho Executive Producer Tomoyuki Tanaka wanted to produce a sequel to the company's 1960 hit *The Human Vapor*, entitled *Frankenstein vs. The Human Vapor*, which was scrapped before it really got going.

But Tanaka still had Frankenstein on the brain, and in 1962 acquired the rights to a project called *King Kong vs. Frankenstein*, which ironically had been originally conceptualized by the original Kong monster maker Willis O'Brien and later co-opted by independent American producer John Beck. This concept would morph into what became *King Kong vs. Godzilla* (1962). The success of that film and how it translated Kong to the Japanese *kaiju* milieu ensured that Toho would remain interested in doing the same with another Western monster staple.

American producer Henry Saperstein, who had transformed UPA from a studio known for innovative theatrical cartoons into a distributor of TV and B-movies, proposed a partnership with Toho to make *Godzilla vs. Frankenstein*. But for whatever reason, the studio balked at using its flagship monster, and instead teamed with Saperstein to pit Godzilla against another Toho creation in *Mothra vs. Godzilla* (1964). Undeterred, UPA continued to work with Toho on a potential Frankenstein project, until something finally began to coalesce in 1965.

Using a concept from screenwriter Takeshi Kimura (writing under his real name, Kaoru Mabuchi) that had begun life as a proposed sequel to *King Kong vs. Godzilla*, a script was crafted with input from American science fiction writer Jerry Sohl and UPA executive producer Reuben Bercovitch. It was an unprecedented level of cooperation between Toho and an American company, intended to directly capitalize on the built-in American audience for these films that had by that time been firmly established. This extended so far as including an American leading man, Nick Adams, as the star of the original Japanese production (rather than insert one in later via re-editing, as had been done in the past).

Adams, best known for his role on TV's *The Rebel*, had been a close friend and collaborator of James Dean. Despite an Oscar nomination for Best Supporting Actor the year before, Adams' Hollywood career had fallen on tough times. In the role of American scientist Dr. James Bowen, he was joined by Kumi Mizuno as his partner and potential love interest, Dr. Sueko Tagami (the duo would work again later that year in Adams' other Toho effort, *Invasion of Astro Monster*, and were rumored to be romantically involved in real life). Adams would also speak his lines in English while the rest of the cast spoke Japanese, with his dialogue dubbed in Japanese for the original release, and restored for the American release.

In the film, Bowen and Tagami discover that the nuclear blast at Hiroshima has somehow caused the irradiated heart of the Frankenstein Monster to regenerate a body, in the form of an odd, mute feral child they discover wandering the city 20 years after the bombing. Taking in the child, they discover he begins to grow at an alarming rate, until he is impossible to contain. The monster, known simply as "Frankenstein" in the movie, is depicted as Caucasian, despite being played by Japanese actor Koji Furuhata, whose real-life hearing and speaking disability lent some aspects of believability to an otherwise far-fetched role. Despite the inability to exactly copy the iconic Frankenstein makeup design created in 1931 by Universal's Jack Pierce, Toho's makeup artists attempted a vague approximation, featuring that unmistakable flat-topped cranium.

Director Ishiro Honda had wanted to explore the creature's pathos and vulnerability, but of course, being a Toho production, there was pressure from Tanaka to incorporate a giant monster battle as well, so a second beast was thrown into the mix—the subterranean-dwelling, horn-headed Baragon, who makes his first of several Toho appearances in this film. The giant-sized Frankenstein inevitably escapes, eventually tangling with Baragon in the film's climactic battle, which sees Frankenstein snap his adversary's neck before both are swallowed-up by an earthquake.

Apparently, this wasn't enough for Saperstein, who also requested that after defeating Baragon, Frankenstein should fight a giant octopus, similar to what King Kong had done in *King Kong vs. Godzilla*.

However, the latter film had used a real octopus, and the prop creature put together this time by Eiji Tsuburaya's monster effects team just didn't meet with Saperstein's approval, and the scene would be shelved, later popping up on a TV version.

The finished product, known in Japan as *Frankenstein vs. Baragon* (1965) but released in the United States a year later as *Frankenstein Conquers the World*, manages to portray a creature that the audience can sympathize with, much like in many other Western interpretations of Frankenstein. There are also a few traces of the original *King Kong vs. Godzilla* sequel script that survive, including Frankenstein's very Kong-like obsession with the beautiful Dr. Tagami. In a trend that demonstrated American distributors' greater confidence in the Toho product by the mid-1960's, the film would be altered very little for the U.S. theatrical release, and was groundbreaking in its Japanese-American collaboration at every stage of production. The film was a success, and would even get a vague sequel in *The War of the Gargantuas* (1966, also covered in this book), although minus Toho's actual Frankenstein creature, which would never be seen again.

Frankenstein Conquers the World was also one of the very last *tokusatsu* or *kaiju* pictures to receive the lavish big-budget treatment from Toho before the science fiction and fantasy stuff would be demoted to the lower budget B-movie division and marketed more directly at children (with 1966's *Godzilla vs. The Sea Monster* usually considered the division point.) As such, it represents a moment in time, when quirky ideas and unchecked creativity still ruled the day at one of the world's leading producers of fantastical entertainment.

1965

JUSTIN HUMPHREYS

Bert I. Gordon's *Village of the Giants* is innocuous in nearly every way: a silly, sophomoric 60's teen comedy variation on H. G. Wells' *The Food of the Gods*. In it—as most of you reading this probably already know—a gang of ultra-square-looking juvenile delinquents (including Beau Bridges, *Coogan's Bluff*'s Tisha Sterling, and *The Rifleman*'s Johnny Crawford) eat experimental "Goop", created by "Genius" (young Ron Howard), which makes them grow enormous. They set themselves up as tinpot dictators of tiny Hainesville, boss around the local Sheriff (Joe Turkel, in-between Kubrick movies), and are eventually deposed in a David-and-Goliath-style confrontation with spunky, twenty-something "teen" Tommy Kirk.

It's a Bert I. Gordon movie, so giant monsters are pretty much inevitable (we cover five of his movies in this book alone), and since this is a comedy, most of them are fairly unintimidating: an oversize cat, dog, and some ducks. The closest thing the movie has to a proper monster is a hulking spider that terrorizes Kirk and his lady love, Nancy (Charla Doherty), in a basement and which Kirk then electrocutes. The creature is unfrightening and winds up obliterated after a couple of minutes onscreen.

The accent in *Village of the Giants* really isn't on monsters, though, unlike so many of Gordon's movies — it's all about Gordon capitalizing on the 60's teen movie wave. Though his *metier* really was giant monster movies, like most drive-in moviemakers, he rode on the coattails of *any* popular genre that came down the pike. When occult horror was big, he directed 1972's *Necromancy*, a horror potboiler with a satanic slant. Ecological science fiction and horror movies emerged as a popular sub-genre, so Gordon made a straight-faced — and even *more* ludicrous — adaptation of *The Food of the Gods* (1976) and a version — arguably, nuttier still! — of Wells' *Empire of the Ants* (1977). When sex comedies exploded in the 80's, he made the bizarre, off-putting *Let's Do It!* (1982). And, with *Village of the Giants*, Gordon was going for a strictly youth audience—the same kids who were flocking to the (better and funnier) *Beach Party* series. The accent here is on Rock 'n' Roll, humor, and titillation, sometimes all at once.

As a director, Gordon never really improved. There are horror and SF filmmakers who, when given tiny budgets, still shined: Gene Fowler, Jr., Edward Cahn, and Curtis Harrington, for starters. Even when saddled with paltry resources and fleeting shooting schedules, there's still a real cinematic spark that's vividly apparent in everything they did. Gordon, however, directed amateurishly early in his career and pretty much stayed amateurish from then on. But, are his films entertaining and worth revisiting? Of course! Would you even be reading this book if they weren't? And why else would I be writing about *Village of the Giants*?

Out of all the movies we're covering here, why would I choose something as relatively indifferent as *Village of the Giants*? One burning reason: it has composer and all-around pop music maestro Jack Nitzsche's first solo movie soundtrack.

You might not recognize Nitzsche's name, but you almost certainly know his work. He was a key member of Phil Spector's "Wall of Sound" gang and had his hands in some of the greatest pop music of the 60's. Among the million songs he worked on, Nitzsche orchestrated The Ronettes' "Be My Baby"; did the choral arrangements on the Rolling Stones' "You Can't Always Get What You Want"; and wrote hits like "Needles and Pins". Like his peers Elmer Bernstein and Burt Bacharach, with *Robot Monster* (1953) and *The Blob* (1958), respectively, few realize that Nitzsche had a drive-in movie in his closet.

Nitzsche's only movie work prior to *Village of the Giants* was playing backup piano for Elvis in *Girls! Girls! Girls!* (1962). After that, he quickly developed into a brilliant, singular film composer, creating unforgettable, eerie, unsettling soundscapes for *Performance* (1970), *One Flew Over the Cuckoo's Nest* (1975), *Hardcore* (1979), and *Cutter's Way* (1981). Other key credits include his properly disturbing music and even sound effects for *The Exorcist* (1973) and *Cruising* (1980). His scores perfectly suited the deeply nasty tone of 70's cinema. The only film music I hold against him is having cowritten probably the worst wedding song ever written: "Up Where We Belong" from *An Officer and a Gentleman* (1982), for which he won his only Oscar.

In the outstanding *Thus Spake Jack Nitzsche* interview series on YouTube, Nitzsche himself derisively recalled his contributions to *Village of the Giants*: "Forget about that one. Someone named Helen Noga, who used to manage Johnny Mathis, wanted to be my manager. So, I said, 'We'll try it for three months.' But she would go around to the movie companies and tell them I was the new Richard Wagner and things like that. It was so embarrassing.

"And out of this, I got *Village of the Giants*. And the reason I got it was because it was a terrible film… I think the score's pretty good but it doesn't fit with the film at all. Actually, that was the first film, but the real first serious film was *Performance*. Mick [Jagger] saw to it that I got that."

Nitzsche wasn't overestimating his work. The jarring thing about his music in *Village of the Giants* is how potent and memorable it is in comparison with everything else about the movie. Nitzsche's marvelous "The Last Race" acts as the film's opening theme and the background track for the "money" scene where the giant delinquents break out into a slow-mo dance. It's a surreal, ridiculous, and incredibly entertaining sequence, climaxing with Johnny Crawford being picked up bodily by Joy Harmon (George Kennedy's "Lucille" from *Cool Hand Luke*) and dangling from gyrating oversized prop cleavage.

Sadly, there was no *Village of the Giants* soundtrack album. A slightly faster-tempo version of "The Last Race", with the sounds of cars revving added, was barely released as a promotional 45 single on Reprise Records. This rare track found new life and exposure as the theme to Quentin Tarantino's *Death Proof* (2007), and was reissued on its soundtrack, then was rereleased again on vinyl on the phenomenal compilation LP, *Jack Nitzsche—The Reprise Singles 1963-1965*.

To me, the "big beast" of *Village of the Giants* isn't the ducks, cat, dog, or spider — or Joy Harmon — it's "The Last Race", or whatever Nitzsche was referring to that track as, at that point. It's a perfect example of his 60's powerhouse rock, pounding away on the soundtrack with its rich, full orchestration. And it's also a key part of what *Village of the Giants* remains significant for, if anything: as a time capsule of that era. It's loaded with period touches, like dancer Toni Basil in a sizable role, usually frugging madly away. There's a sequence where the kids all head to the Sunset Strip's Whisky A Go Go — miraculously transported from L.A. to this backwater town! — to see The Beau Brummels perform. And then there's a giant miscreant reading an issue of *Famous Monsters of Filmland* with Gordon's *War of the Colossal Beast* (see earlier chapter) on the cover. (*Famous Monsters* editor Forry Ackerman visited the film's set and, Forry being Forry, had his picture taken alongside the disembodied Kong-sized breasts.)

None of the criticisms I've made are to dismiss *Village of the Giants'* watchability. It's not a deathless wonder of American cinema, but it lingers in the memory. And here we are discussing it sixty years after its original release. Not all drive-in movies are lucky enough to be remembered, and only one — this one — was fortunate enough to bear Jack Nitzsche's extraordinary stamp.

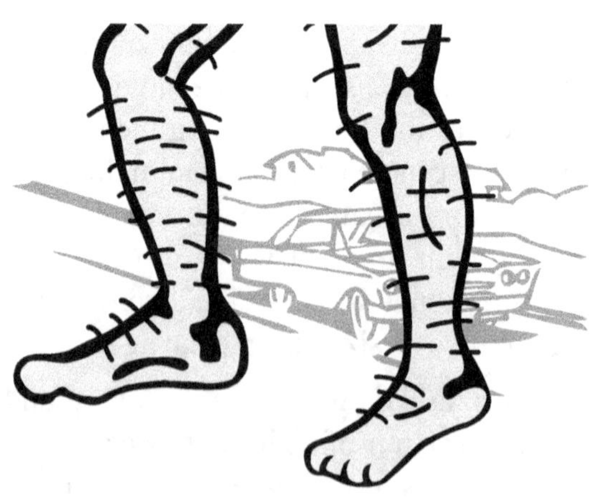

THE WAR OF THE GARGANTUAS

1966/1970

BRIAN R. SOLOMON

When a movie is a favorite of people like Brad Pitt, Quentin Tarantino, Nicolas Cage, and Guillermo del Toro, who are we to argue? *The War of the Gargantuas* is among Toho's most beloved *kaiju* (giant monster) films—especially the ones without "Godzilla" in the title—and has been cherished for decades by the baby boomers and Gen-Xers who first discovered it in the 1970's. A quirky, colorful and surreal monster movie, it started life as a vague, unofficial sequel to Toho's *Frankenstein Conquers the World* (aka *Frankenstein vs. Baragon*, see earlier chapter), but morphed into something that stands on its own two (or four) hairy, clawed feet and is more than worthy of attention for anyone claiming to be a *kaiju* aficionado.

The final Japanese-American collaboration between Toho Studios and Henry J. Saperstein's UPA, the movie began life as *Furankenshutain no Kaijū: Sanda tai Gaira* (*Frankenstein's Monsters: Sanda vs. Gaira*), with a script by the previous film's screenwriter Takeshi Kimura, once again putting that old warhorse of Japanese *tokusatsu* (special effects) cinema, Ishiro Honda, in the director's chair. But by 1966, the so-called "Kaiju Boom" in Japan was already beginning to decline, and budgets were being slashed. Toho Executive Producer Tomoyuki Tanaka had canceled Honda's contract and put him on a per-movie deal. More than ever, the money coming in from UPA was needed, and Saperstein was very heavily involved in the production.

One of Saperstein's decisions was to ditch American leading man Nick Adams, who had starred in *Frankenstein Conquers the World* (as well as *Invasion of Astro Monster* aka *Monster Zero*) the same year, in favor of Russ Tamblyn, known at the time for prestigious American pictures like *Seven Brides for Seven Brothers* (1954), *Peyton Place* (1957), *Cimarron* (1960), *The Haunting* (1963) and most notably *West Side Story* (1961). Predictably, however, Tamblyn was notoriously difficult on set, taking great issue with Kimura's script and his dialogue, choosing instead to make up his own dialogue, much to the chagrin and frustration of Honda, who was attempting to cope with him through an exasperated Japanese translator.

Although the disgruntled Tamblyn does seem to sleepwalk through his role, the movie is a whole lot more fun than the Oscar-nominated actor would allow himself to view it. It may be a far cry from Robert Wise, Jerome Robbins, and Leonard Bernstein, but how could you not love a movie that opens with a gigantic green-haired humanoid fighting a giant octopus and destroying a boat? Or that features a resort lounge singer played by Carol Burnett's sister-in-law getting eaten by the same creature shortly after finishing her song (the unforgettable and prophetic "The Words Get Stuck in My Throat")?

In the original Japanese version, the first green giant who shows up is suspected by the Japanese government to be the Frankenstein monster seen in the previous film, thought to be destroyed. But Tamblyn's Dr. Paul Stewart and his partner Dr. Akemi Togawa (reprising her role from the first movie, kind of) insist their creature was too peaceful. Later, when a more friendly brown-haired humanoid giant shows up to rescue the green-haired one, we learn that it's that one which is the original Frankenstein (despite looking nothing like it), and the destructive green-haired monster is actually a clone of the original, grown from cellular matter that drifted out to sea after the events of the first movie and was somehow nurtured by plankton and the nutrients in the ocean. The green and brown-haired beings are given the respective names Gaira and Sanda, for no apparent reason, and the rest of the movie builds to their inevitable battle, during which both appear to be destroyed in a volcanic eruption.

The creature designs created by the special effects unit of *tokusatsu* legend Eiji Tsuburaya, aided by his eventual replacement Teruyoshi

Nakano, are unusual for a Toho film in their humanoid appearance, and result in a lot of mobility during the movie's memorable fight scenes. Suit actor Haruo Nakajima, who played Gaira but is best known as the man in the Godzilla suit for years, later cited this movie as his favorite because of how expressive the costume allowed him to be, including showing his own eyes for the first and only time.

The Frankenstein connection in the movie is explained in a pretty flimsy way, and the real connection to the original is sometimes confusing and inaccurate, leading one to assume that they were never that committed to it in the first place. For example, Tamblyn and Mizuno are clearly supposed to be the two scientists from *Frankenstein Conquers the World*... yet their characters have different names. There's also a flashback scene showing them caring for their Frankenstein creature when he was a child, purportedly showing events from the previous movie... yet in the original film, the young Frankenstein is a human-looking child with the trademark flat-topped head, whereas in the flashback it's depicted as a furry, ape-like creature that looks nothing like it.

But if you don't let these things bother you—which is highly advised—it's easy to understand why this movie became such a cult classic. Perhaps sensing the Frankenstein confusion, when Saperstein oversaw the editing and production of the film for its American release, he had all references to Frankenstein and the events of the first film removed from the dialogue, instead retitling the now-standalone movie as *The War of the Gargantuas* and having the creatures referred to as "gargantuas" throughout. Discovering that Tamblyn's original English dialogue track had been somehow lost after production of the Japanese version, Saperstein had a reluctant Tamblyn come into a studio to re-record it—the problem was, no script was provided, and the actor was required to base his lines on lip-reading all his scenes, further hampering his already somnambulant performance in the film.

Despite his efforts, or perhaps because of them, Saperstein had difficulty selling his movie to American distributors, and it wasn't until 1970—four years after the Japanese release—that it finally hit US theaters as part of a double-bill with another Saperstein co-produced Toho orphan, *Monster Zero*.

And although Saperstein may not have expected it, there were plenty of kids enthralled by the strange movie, and those kids would go on to become important people in the industry. Brad Pitt has cited it as the first movie he ever saw, and called it a transformative experience for him on a live Oscars broadcast. Quentin Tarantino based the fight between Uma Thurman and Daryl Hannah in *Kill Bill 2* on the fight between Sanda and Gaira, and the word "gargantuan" is even conspicuously used several times in the movie. Guillermo del Toro cited the movie as an influence on his 2013 *kaiju* mash-up *Pacific Rim*. And even the song "The Words Get Stuck in My Throat" became a cult favorite, covered by bands like Devo and sung in a cheeky *Gargantuas* parody in an episode of the animated 2010's series *Scooby-Doo! Mystery Incorporated* entitled, "Battle of the Humungonauts".

For a movie without any of Toho's more iconic monsters like Godzilla, Mothra, Rodan, et al, *The War of the Gargantuas* is a picture with a whole lot of pop culture cache. In fact, Michael Dougherty, director and writer of Legendary Pictures' *Godzilla: King of the Monsters* (2019) and writer of Legendary's *Godzilla vs. Kong* (2021) has even theorized about bringing the Gargantuas into Legendary's MonsterVerse franchise in the future if given the chance. But whether or not Sanda and Gaira ever get their day in the spotlight once again, the original film remains one of the most downright enjoyable giant monster movies ever made.

KING KONG ESCAPES

1967/1968

BRIAN R. SOLOMON

The most unusual and overlooked film in the entire 90-year King Kong franchise, *King Kong Escapes* is a fascinating oddity that combines the Japanese *kaiju* (giant monster) cinematic approach with a strong American influence in a movie that is squarely aimed at children, to the point of even being based on a Saturday morning kid's cartoon series. It would actually mark the second time that Japan's Toho Studio had taken a crack at Kong, but to make matters even more convoluted, this film has no connection at all to Toho's previous effort, *King Kong vs. Godzilla* (1962), other than the fact that the two movies were produced by the same company.

A fantastical story that places Kong firmly on the side of the good guys, *King Kong Escapes* also features the first live action mecha (giant robot) ever seen in Japan, in the form of the formidable Mechani-Kong that serves as the nemesis to the Eighth Wonder of the World. Mechani-Kong predates even Mechagodzilla, and would lead the way for all sorts of giant mechanized heroes and menaces in Japanese film, TV, and anime from *Gundam* to *Robotech* to American crossovers like *Transformers* and the work of Japanese-influenced Western filmmakers such as Guillermo del Toro's *Pacific Rim*.

The film was the product of a pairing between Toho and American animation studio Rankin-Bass. Toho had previously had success teaming with American outfits like American International Pictures (AIP) and United Productions of America (UPA), and could use the influx of cash, as the golden age of Japanese *tokusatsu* (special effects) cinema, and Japanese cinema in general, was winding down thanks to the popularity of television, and studios were hungry for funding.

Toho had been interested in revisiting Kong ever since the success of *King Kong vs. Godzilla*, but no longer had the license to the character, which was owned at the time by Universal. Rankin-Bass had been producing the animated TV series *The King Kong Show* starting in 1966, and were no strangers to Japanese partnership, as they worked with Japanese animation house Toei Studio on the series, and had worked with Japanese animators on their now-beloved series of holiday-themed, stop-motion TV specials like *Rudolph the Red-Nosed Reindeer* (1964). Toho wanted a new Kong picture, and Rankin-Bass wanted a live action spinoff of their cartoon; it seemed to be a perfect match.

However, their first planned collaboration, a movie that would see Kong do battle with a giant sea creature on a tropical island, fell through when the two companies couldn't agree on personnel. Rankin-Bass insisted on Toho's top *tokusatsu* director, Ishiro Honda, and the legendary special effects director Eiji Tsuburaya. But Toho was in the midst of downgrading its *tokusatsu* and *kaiju* pictures to its B-movie division, and had instead pegged less proven director Jun Fukuda to direct, and assigned Tsuburaya's apprentice Sadamasa Arikawa to do the special effects. Rankin-Bass wound up backing out of the project, leading Toho to switch out King Kong for Godzilla, with the finished product becoming *Ebirah, Horror of the Deep*, aka *Godzilla vs. The Sea Monster* (1966).

Thankfully, the two companies were able to come back to the bargaining table the following year—Rankin-Bass got Ishiro Honda and Eiji Tsuburaya as they wanted, and Toho was finally able to bring King Kong back to the big screen. The movie, known in Japan as *Kingu Kongu no gyakushu* (roughly translated as King Kong's Revenge), would be very loosely based on *The King Kong Show* cartoon series. The idea of a benevolent Kong living on a tropical island and befriended by humans would remain, although the human characters would change. The villain in the film, Dr. Who (no connection to the popular British sci-fi series, although it's been noted the character design bears a striking resemblance to William Hartnell's original version of The Doctor as seen on the BBC from 1963 to 1966) is taken from the cartoon series. And Mechani-Kong was first seen on *The King Kong Show* as well, although the robot looked quite a bit different.

As had been done in other Toho collaborations with American companies, the cast would be a combination of Japanese and American actors. The lantern-jawed Rhodes Reason, veteran of TV and B-movies, would be brought in to play submarine commander Carl Nelson. Reason would later recall the production in a very negative light, criticizing what he characterized as Toho's amateurish and hackneyed methods of filmmaking and storytelling, and apparently seeing the whole thing as beneath him, despite the fact that even a cursory perusal of his general body of work would indicate otherwise. Mie Hama, previously seen in *King Kong vs. Godzilla* and fresh off playing Bond girl Kissy Suzuki alongside Sean Connery in *You Only Live Twice* (1967), appears as the mysterious Madame Piranha (Madame X in the American version). Linda Jo Miller, an American model working in Japan, was hired to play Lt. Susan Watson, even dying her hair blond to better fit the "damsel in distress" trope established by Fay Wray in the original *King Kong*.

Incorporating elements of the spy and espionage films popular at the time and typified by the Bond series, the plot entails Madame X, representing a hostile unnamed nation heavily hinted to be North Korea, hiring Dr. Who (played by veteran character actor Hideyo Amamoto) to build Mechani-Kong in order to mine at the North Pole for the coveted Element X. When the robot fails, Who captures the real thing and tries to enslave the beast. The whole thing culminates in a battle in Tokyo between the robot and the gorilla, even including a climb up Tokyo Tower, deliberately suggesting the Empire State Building climax from the '33 film.

The Japanese version was released in July of 1967, with the American version put together by Rankin-Bass and distributed 11 months later by Universal Pictures, the owners of the King Kong copyright. Reason was brought in to re-record all his English dialogue, while Miller unfortunately was not—a result of Reason being a SAG member. Miller would strongly disapprove of the stilted, somewhat grating tones of voice actress Julie Bennett, and her actual voice isn't heard in either version of the film. The majority of the rest of the male voices would be done by the illustrious and ubiquitous Paul Frees, Rankin-Bass's in-house voice maestro responsible for so many voices for characters in their TV specials of the 1960's and 1970's.

Toho always had a great love for King Kong, in some ways the original movie *kaiju*. They attempted to bring the big ape back for the epic *Destroy All Monsters* in 1968, but their rights to the character had lapsed and so he was replaced by Gorosaurus, ironically a *kaiju* introduced in *King Kong Escapes* as another foil for the Eighth Wonder. Decades later, Toho would attempt to make *Godzilla vs. Mechani-Kong* and found they weren't even allowed to do *that*, instead turning the project into *Godzilla vs. King Ghidorah* (1991)… which just so happened to include a Mecha-King Ghidorah.

It was not until the modern-day Legendary Godzilla series that Kong would once again appear alongside a Japanese *kaiju* in a film distributed by Toho (at least in Japan), *Godzilla vs. Kong* (2021). But nothing could take the place of the innocence and child-like wonder of *King Kong Escapes*, a movie tailor-made for a juvenile audience that is grossly underserved by the giant beast cinema of the present day.

1969

STEVEN PEROS

For those who complain about poor English dubbing in Japanese monster movies, no such issue exists in *Latitude Zero*. It is the first and last film from the combined forces of Toho Studios and their legendary *Godzilla* director, Ishiro Honda, to be shot in Japan with a Japanese and American cast, but spoken entirely in English from an English-language script by an American screenwriter (for more on Honda, see chapters on *Half Human*, *King Kong vs Godzilla*, *The War of the Gargantuas*, *Frankenstein Conquers the World*, and *King Kong Escapes*). It was a big financial risk, but one Toho felt they had to take to keep up with the rising demands of competing in the international marketplace.

A year earlier, one of Toho's lesser competitors, Toei, had partnered with MGM in the US for their all-English-speaking *Alien*-esque space opera, *The Green Slime*, so before that film hit the theatrical marketplace, Toho partnered with US producer/financier Ambassador Productions for screenwriter, Ted Sherderman, to adapt his own 1941 radio serial, *Latitude Zero*, into a special effects-driven feature film. Unfortunately, midway through production, Ambassador failed to keep up paying their half of the million-dollar budget. The costs were slashed and Toho footed the remainder of the bill, purportedly reducing the total budget to $800,000.

The chief link between Toei's *The Green Slime* and Toho's *Latitude Zero* is the always likable Richard Jaeckel (1976's *Grizzly*) whose career started at age 16 in 1943's box office hit, *Guadalcanal Diary*, and lasted for fifty years, including a Best Supporting Actor Oscar nomination. Here, he plays Perry Lawton, a cocky photojournalist for Transglobe News sent out on the research vessel, Fuji, to investigate something called the Cromwell Current which, if properly utilized, could increase the speed of submarines. Together with oceanographer, Dr. Ken Tashiro (Akira Takarada, veteran of six *Godzilla* movies as well *Half Human* and *King Kong Escapes*) and geologist, Dr. Jules Masson (Japanese -Danish actor, Masumi Okada), the three men board a diving bell which is dropped at Latitude Zero (the intersection of the Equator and the International Date Line). As their vessel descends to the ocean floor, an undersea earthquake occurs, providing the first of several impressive special effects sequences, including spectacular multi-color explosions that erupt out of the ocean and fill the sky above. Ultimately, the three men are knocked unconscious.

Upon awakening, the trio find themselves aboard the super-mod, high-tech submarine, Alpha, under the advanced medical care of scantily clad Dr. Anne Barton (the screen debut of 20-year-old, Florida-born, Linda Haynes), whose very presence reduces all three men to leering teenage boys. They soon meet their host, Captain Craig McKenzie (*Citizen Kane*'s Joseph Cotton) whose silky, revealing outfits, and those of his crew, can best be described as something the Village People might have worn on a 1976 field-trip to Studio 54. The New York Times' review was less sensitive, describing the movie's overall decor as "fruity" (Hey, I didn't write it; I'm just quoting the world's "newspaper of record"). McKenzie and his vessel are a sort of peace-loving twist on Captain Nemo, living off the sea and welcoming scientists and dignitaries who wish to trade in man's landlocked rat-race for the domed undersea utopia McKenzie has created, called Latitude Zero. Among its many virtues is the ability to slow down the aging process. Not only does McKenzie claim to be 204 years old, but his one enemy is former college classmate, Dr. Malic (Cesar Romero, best known as The Joker from TV's *Batman*), who is 203!

Malic, whose prime form of communication is an endless supply of evil grimaces and sadistic cackles, is master of a private island fortress within the dome, patrolled by his own high-tech submarine, Black Shark. At Malic's side are two women who lust for him: Lucretia (veteran actress, Patricia Medina, who was also the wife of Joseph Cotton) and Captain Kuroiga (Hikaru Kuroki). Though their desire is unrequited (after all, Malic can only truly love the chaos he creates), he keeps both women on short leashes so he can use them to do his bidding, starting with Captain Kuroiga, who helms Black Shark and engages Alpha in what may be cinema's first and only high speed submarine chase, the movie's second marvelously detailed effects sequence. Alpha ultimately prevails, entering the portal to Latitude Zero and emerging into its domed bay, impressively presented via a combination of wonderful miniatures and matte paintings, supervised by Toho special effects legend, Eiji Tsubaraya (responsible for all of Toho's special effects from 1954's *Godzilla* up until his death in 1970).

All paths collide when Dr. Okada (Tetsu Nakamura) and his daughter, Tsuruko (Mari Nakayama) are kidnapped from their ship by Malic. Dr. Okada has invented a serum to immunize against radiation and Malic wants it for his nefarious purposes. When Dr. Okada refuses (at just shy of the movie's one-hour mark), we finally get our first glimpse of giant beasts. Malic runs a sort of *Island of Dr. Moreau* and has at his disposal man-sized bats which he has created in his lab! But the movie's truly heavyweight giant beast comes when Malic realizes that McKenzie and the visiting trio are planning to infiltrate his domain to rescue the doctor. So naturally, Malic subdues a lion, sews on the wings of an eagle, inserts loyal Captain Kurioga's brain, uses a beam to grow the creature to giant beast proportions, and —voila! — the perfect weapon to defeat the intruders.

Unfortunately, Malic failed to take into account that when you murder someone who loves you and put their brain in the body of a giant beast with claws and fangs, they may just rip you to shreds instead of your enemy, which is exactly what happens. Ultimately, MacKenzie & Company do battle with man-sized rats, storm Malic's lair, do laser-battle with his flying bat-men, save the doctor and his daughter, and blow up Malic's evil private island. Of the three visitors, only reporter, Perry Lawton, chooses to return to the surface to tell the tale. His life-raft is rescued by a US Naval Ship and in a confounding final riff on *The Wizard of Oz*, Lawton is shocked to see that the Captain and his two officers are the spitting images of McKenzie, Malic, and his oceanographer buddy, Ken. What's more, all of Lawton's film is blank and his tobacco bag, which he had filled with 600 carats of the diamonds that are plentiful on Latitude Zero, is now filled with tobacco once again. He is thought quite mad, until a telegram comes to the ship for Lawton saying that 600 carats of diamonds were delivered to him. Ah! So it's all true or… huh? This head-scratcher of an ending makes no sense no matter how you slice it, though please feel free to debate it with your friends.

Latitude Zero has a mixed rep largely because the movie itself is a mixed bag of extremes, such as its gorgeous production design versus its tacky costume design. This is further exemplified by its special effects, which suffered once the budget was slashed. So, while the miniatures, explosions, subs, and matte paintings are wonderful, the giant monsters are at the level of men dressed up in furry costumes to entertain children at a birthday party. But even here, *Latitude Zero* has a certain jaw-droppingly insane charm, as does its mash-up of tones (is it Pacifist Sci-Fi? Tough Action-Adventure? Grotesque Mad-Scientist Horror? Innocent Children's Fantasy?) but there's one thing for certain: given the identity crisis of genres fused into one colorful, English-language, Japanese-American widescreen co-production, you'll never see two movies like *Latitude Zero*.

Also from BearManor Media

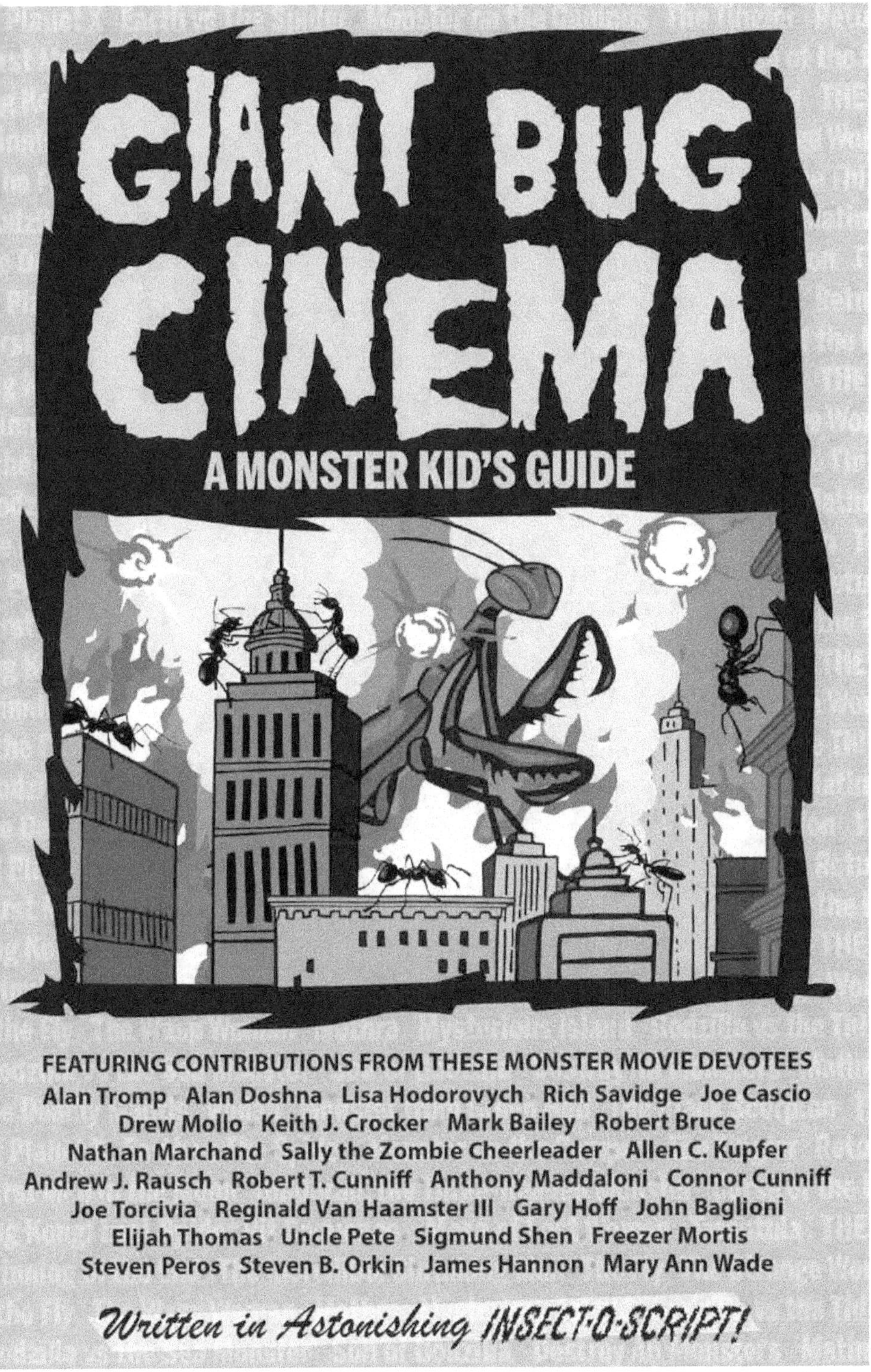